Deep Agroecology

Farms, Food, and Our Future

Deep Agroecology

Farms, Food, and Our Future

Steven McFadden

LIGHT AND SOUND PRESS
www.lightandsoundpress.com

Deep Agroecology: Farms, Food, and Our Future
© 2019 by Steven McFadden

ISBN: 978-1-7923-0928-1
Library of Congress Control Number: 2019912060

Light and Sound Press
Lincoln, Nebraska
www.lightandsoundpress.com

Cover design: Angela Werneke, River Light Media,
Santa Fe, New Mexico
Page design and layout: Cris Trautner and Aaron Vacin,
Infusionmedia, Lincoln, Nebraska

For Elizabeth

Contents

"This is just the beginning of our work."

— Eduardo Rincón

Introduction

"The way of life known as Western Civilization is on a death path... Our essential message to the world is a basic call to consciousness. The destruction of native cultures and people is the same process which has destroyed and is destroying life on this planet."

—Basic Call to Consciousness,
Haudenosaunee elders

Having heard the call to consciousness of our native relatives here in North America, I propose that *deep agroecology* can and must be among our intelligent and heartfelt responses. The union of native wisdom ways with the sophisticated, sustainable tools and techniques of Western civilization is a process that can—and necessarily must—lead to the renewal and elevation of all forms of life on this continent and planet. The key to this union and renewal lies in the realm of farms and food. Deep agroecology is a concept intended to help turn that key, allowing us to enter more fully into the potentialities that lie within individuals and communities. It's imperative that we do so.

I write for all, not just for farmers. The challenges we face are beyond the capacity of that small segment of our population, about 1 percent in North America. The challenges require us all to step up to higher, more inspired, and dramatically cleaner and stronger systems of tending the land and growing the food that sustains us. We must do it together. Farms are the foundation of our civilization. That civilization is fragmenting. In light of this reality, we must be about the work of building a new agrarian foundation. This is a high and urgent mission for the Americas and for the world.

I'm neither a farmer nor a scholar, but rather a journalist with a special interest in the health of the Earth and all which shares life upon it. In deep agroecology I see an essential story, a story that can inform the general public about the agricultural issues underlying so many of our current challenges and the creative, healing agroecological pathways people are establishing in response. With the theme of deep agroecology I hope to anchor those understandings more firmly throughout the Americas by showing how the deepest roots of our land can help support the agriculture that undergirds the whole of our culture.

Agrarian idealism has a long history, dating back many millennia in native communities around the globe, and in the West at least as far back as the Roman empire. The agrarian vision has been expressed eloquently in American letters through the writings of figures such as Thomas Jefferson, Henry David Thoreau, Victor Davis Hanson, Mary Hunter Austin, John Crowe Ransom, Barbara Kingsolver, and a great many others.

In 1915, for example, Liberty Hyde Bailey wrote *The Holy Earth*. Hyde had served as the dean of agriculture at Cornell University and eventually came to be known as the "Father of Modern Horticulture." Like so many other people in the lineage of agrarian visionaries, he had a clear understanding of agriculture as the foundation for a spiritually elevated way of life, and he expressed that in his book. In that sense, the vision offered through the concept of deep agroecology is not new but rather my effort to report upon and thereby add fresh impetus to the ancient and honorable agrarian wisdom stream. We need that stream now more than ever before.

*   *   *

My intention in writing *Deep Agroecology* is to explain to a general audience what agroecology already is and to embed the concepts and practices more purposefully in the public mind, while offering emphasis to a subtle dimension of it, a realm of critical mystery. Another reason for writing is to again make available, as many communicators have done through the millennia, a reminder that inspiriting yourself and then caring actively for the Earth, the sustenance we derive from it, and the communities we are part of, is a high, noble, and heroic calling. It's especially gallant at this juncture of time and circumstance.

Our entire relationship to the Earth and our specific environments is being challenged. Agroecology and deep agroecology are intelligent, sophisticated, practical, and effective ways to meet and transcend those challenges, establishing a clean, healthy foundation on the Earth for the next evolutionary step of humanity. We can respond wisely and decisively to the chaos in our climate and culture, for the present and for the future. Toward that end, this book assembles a chorus of voices and a pastiche of related and relevant facts, experiences, ideas, and ideals. Together they describe a whole: the vibrant agroecological vision that is arising in the Americas and around the world, a vision that merits clarification and amplification. That's another facet of my intention for *Deep Agroecology*.

Agroecology is a concept that has been refined in recent decades, developed, and made ready for wide global implementation. It's new territory for many, but natural territory. Farmers cannot enter this territory successfully alone, though. They must be accompanied in various purposeful ways by the communities and households who receive their bounty and who take it into their bodies.

Although to date the term has not been widely used or understood in America, agroecology has become a buzzword and a leading-edge concept internationally. The basic idea, the spirit of agroecology, is an approach to farming and food that is clean, sustainable, humane, egalitarian, and just, rooted in ecology, other sciences, and indigenous knowledge. The concepts and approaches of agroecology can mean many things, though some who claim the term use practices that diverge from the spirit. Our precarious circumstances call upon us to engage and to clarify the term agroecology so that its principles and practices hold true and helpful meaning. To meet the daunting challenges of our era, we must actively employ this knowledge with high dedication and skill.

The concept of deep agroecology—and the challenge to write a book about it—was presented to me several years ago by Chuck Francis, professor of agronomy, agroecology, crop rotations, and farming systems at the University of Nebraska–Lincoln (UNL). One early September morning in 2012 I was tending to the front yard of our home at the time, not far from UNL's East Campus. I was standing with a rake in my hands, pruning shears belted to my hips, sizing up the work that needed to be done. That's when Chuck came by on his bike, pedaling his way to East Campus, as he did routinely. He stopped to chat. In the midst of our conversation, he offered me what I've come to think of as a kind of Zen koan, or perhaps I should call it an ag koan. A koan is a proposition intended to provoke questioning, contemplation, and eventually (perhaps) enlightenment.

"Have you ever given any thought to writing a book about deep agroecology?" Professor Francis asked. Now that was an arresting question. Never heard of such a thing. What is *deep agroecology?* And if I knew what it was, what could I possibly say about it that would amount to a worthwhile contribution? I've needed to live with Chuck's ag koan for about seven years to get beyond a glimmer. From the steadily intensifying conviction that I might learn something of value and then communicate it, the idea of this book germinated.

In my conception, deep agroecology is our next natural, intelligent, and necessary evolutionary step. Deep agroecology arises from recognition that the way we farm the land will determine the destiny of life on the Earth. As a philosophy and an approach, deep agroecology strives to marry the subtle spiritual realities of human beings and planet Earth into a balanced relationship with the gross physical realities of farms, technology, food, and flesh. Deep agroecology is a philosophical guide to survival, with intimations of destiny and activation of our spiritual potential as individual human beings who are among the collective inhabitants of our Earth.

Deep agroecology might also be thought of as spiritually intelligent agriculture. By that I do not necessarily mean religiously smart agriculture. In my understanding, spirit far transcends the boundaries of our human-devised religious systems for attempting to give it expression. The religions of the world are not the spirit of the world, rather they are some of the conduits and vessels.

Having said that, it's important to acknowledge that many religious institutions are creatively practicing their faith by working steadily and progressively to pioneer farm and food systems that are just and sustainable. In this manner they are among those communities and institutions expressing the leading edge of what I am calling deep agroecology, and they are worthy of honor and support.

For the purposes of this book, I want to reach beyond the institutional level, to embrace all respectful forms for approaching mystery, no matter the label attached to the form. Readers will note that I've chosen to express the concept of mystery as a common noun. To capitalize the word as a proper noun would ratify a false distinction between spirit, mystery, and the rocks, trees, cows, corn, beans, and human beings who populate the world. All dwell amid an interwoven unified field. For deep agroecology, this is an intrinsic understanding.

My intention for this book is that it helps inspire and coalesce efforts to establish an agrarian foundation for spiritual activation. Nothing less will do. The single-minded materialist view and mode of thinking is inadequate to the challenges we face, and often toxic or counterproductive to evolution. Expressions of deep agroecology are an essential evolutionary step for all the peoples of the Americas—South, Central, and North—as well as for all the world.

In my life I've walked long miles on both agrarian and native pathways and have had the opportunity to form many friendships and learn great lessons. This book is an opportunity for me to bring those pathways to a dynamic crossroads. The cultures that have streamed onto North America have never fully connected with respect to the rootstock cultures that have been on this continent (Turtle Island) for 18,000 years or more. It's past time for that to change. My hope is that the agrarian crossroads depicted in this book will support the development of that relationship.

Planetary deterioration confronts us all. We are all challenged to respond intelligently and effectively as we see the deserts relentlessly growing, the poles melting, the seas rising, and climate chaos delivering blows near and far. The farming systems that yield our food not only affect our health through diet but also through the environment. Farms may serve either as engines of pollution or as oases of radiant environmental health. Those healing oases around the globe are being established through agroecology.

Over the last 40 years, I've witnessed the increasing mechanization, chemicalization, genetic manipulation, industrialization, and corporate consolidation of the culture that produces the food we all eat—agriculture. I came to feel that I must sound a voice in counterpoint, a voice for a higher, more spiritually sustaining system for our land, for our farmers, for our food, and for our culture.

This book was not produced under the illusion that I know more or that I possess acumen beyond what our academies and the pioneers of ecology, deep ecology, and agroecology have already gained in experience, knowledge, and wisdom. Nor have I the arrogance to imagine I possess more than a glimpse of native wisdom ways or that I love the land any more deeply than the farmers who cultivate it. I know only enough to have gained respect and appreciation for all the pathways of wisdom now available.

A principal goal of this book is in fact to help educate the general public about these many pathways of knowledge and practice and to encourage active engagement. I see places where these knowings may be intentionally and beneficially joined for the present and the future at a cultural crossroads. The philosophical and practical rootstocks of the Americas can anchor and inform the sophisticated, sustainable, clean, and radiant technologies arising out of the multitude of cultures that have come to the Americas from around the world.

*   *   *

Delivered to the United Nations in 1977, *The Haudenosaunee Address to the Western World* remains acutely relevant. The message of the address was later published in book form, *Basic Call to Consciousness*, with chapters titled "Thoughts of Peace: Our Strategy for Survival" and "Spiritualism: The Highest Form of Political Consciousness."

In their address the elders said, "The commodification of nature: land, water, and air, casts everything in a different light, a light that is not healthy and cannot sustain over generations... The people who are living on this planet need to break with the narrow concept of human liberation, and begin to see liberation as something which needs to be extended to the whole of the Natural World. What is needed is the liberation of all the things that support Life—the air, the waters, the trees—all the things which support the sacred web of Life...."

Many of the native elders whom I've known and conversed with over the years encourage people to cultivate and maintain positive spiritual thought and to focus on individual and collective internal order. As I've heard them express it, our efforts to bring changes through laws, regulations, and activism can only succeed when we have developed an honest spiritual coherence that includes respect for other people, other spiritual outlooks, and all of the natural world.

My gift as a writer has been the ability to unite: to weave together many voices to create a coherent whole. This is a fitting skill set for the proposed task of this book: defining and exploring the concept of deep agroecology.

My methodology in writing has been to gather wide input from people, publications, and my own direct experience in gardens, farm fields, orchards, forests, vineyards, and lecture halls. I then reflected upon that input, striving to synthesize that it might be given expression in plain language accessible to all readers. If I have contributed any original ideas as this book has evolved, then they are mainly in the realm of linkages, connecting threads among ideas and practices that others have birthed and communicated to create the socially, morally, environmentally, and spiritually informed matrix that I describe as deep agroecology. I have endeavored to give proper acknowledgment to all these contributions.

Over the span of human history, a lot of creative people have applied their minds and hearts to the fundamental challenge of feeding themselves and their communities in a bountiful manner and to making a good life for all. This book rests on their aspirations and contributions.

Chapter 1

Right Names

"The beginning of wisdom is to call things by their right names."

—Confucius

Truth actually exists, whereas falsehood is fiction. Falsehood can for a time obscure truth, but eventually—because truth is real and falsehoods are by their very definition unreal—the natural, inherent power of truth comes forward. This metaphysical absolute was long ago realized and acknowledged in the ancient root language of Sanskrit. In Sanskrit the term *satyagraha* ("truth force") expresses the fundamental spiritual realization that truth is inevitable. Ultimately, beyond every lie, misunderstanding, falsehood, or obscuration, truth exists as reality.

The term satyagraha was also used to characterize a form of nonviolent civil resistance under the leadership of Mahatma Gandhi (1869–1948). Gandhi, the activist and spiritual leader who led India to independence from British colonial rule, recognized that when people align themselves with truth power, they find a natural energy to help move their causes forward.

Former US Vice President Al Gore recognized that natural power too. He brought appreciation for satyagraha to public attention via the speech he gave when he was awarded the Nobel Peace Prize in 2007, as well as through his films about climate change, *An Inconvenient Truth* (2006) and *An Inconvenient Sequel: Truth to Power* (2017).

One truth I regard as relentlessly evident is the looming reality that we must now make a meaningful stride forward in our maturity as human beings. In this process of maturation, our relationships with land, farms, and food are fundamental. Agriculture—the indispensable foundation of all culture—is the great factor. It's also the great opportunity.

Most of what I have to say in this book depends less on my powers of documentation, explanation, and argumentation and far more on you, the reader, and your interest in peering more deeply into what is going on and questioning what we might do to place ourselves on a healthy, technologically adept, and spiritually sophisticated agrarian trajectory. That kind of awakening is necessary as a matter of survival.

With all of that in mind, along with Confucius's counsel on the beginning of wisdom, here in my conception are right names for some of the critical factors bearing upon our farms, our food, and our well-being. They mark the trail for exploring industrial agriculture, agroecology, and deep agroecology.

Anthropocene—This is the term now widely used to describe the geological epoch we are living in, as opposed to earlier periods that have been given names such as Pleistocene, Miocene, or Holocene. The *Anthropocene* epoch is one in which human agency is affecting the planet as much as or more than any natural force. The term derives from ancient Greek: *anthropo* for "man" and *cene* for "new."

The Anthropocene is happening right now. Through industrialization and other human activities, we are making disturbingly powerful and noticeable impacts on our planet's geology and ecosystems. Our industries and our predations have caused mass extinctions of great numbers of plant and animal species, polluted the oceans, and altered the atmosphere, among other lasting impacts. We have changed—and are changing—geological history.

If we human beings can change the condition of the Earth, as we have demonstrated with our extracting and polluting industries, then we also have the potential to change it in clean, positive, sustainable, life-radiant ways.

Climate Chaos—This is the right name for the hard reality concerning what climate change is actually doing to our planetary support systems. The acceleration in the number of and frequency of documented climate-related, ultra-extreme weather events is dramatic. Charts showing the rate of temperature change in polar regions and the world's primary farming areas are stunning. With all that's going on in the world, I suppose climate change can seem at times like mere background noise unless it is directly impacting your life. But it's not background. It's real, it's here, it's intensifying, and we and our children and grandchildren will contend with the impact for decades to come.

Climate chaos is a driving force behind the breakup of the North and South Poles, sea-level shifts, massive flooding events, droughts, resource wars, record-shattering storms, widespread migration of insect pests and diseases, waves of human refugees, and more. We ignore climate realities at great peril. Agroecology and deep agroecology are ways to face the reality with sophisticated intelligence grounded in Earth wisdom ways.

A landmark 2018 report from the UN's Intergovernmental Panel on Climate Change (IPCC) described the harsh realities of climate change consequences already impacting us, building in intensity, and soon to be raging by 2040, a period well within the lifetime of much of the global population. The IPCC report specifically depicts a world of worsening food shortages, droughts, floods, wildfires, and mass die-off of coral reefs, which help sustain life in the oceans. Avoiding or minimizing the damage, the report said, requires transforming the world economy at a speed and scale that has "no documented historic precedent."

According to a 2018 report from the UN's Food and Agriculture Organization (FAO), the pattern is established. Extreme heat, droughts, floods, and storms have doubled since the early 1990s, an average of 213 of these events occurring every year during the period of 1990 to 2016. These extreme disasters hinder agricultural productivity, resulting in food price hikes, hunger, and income losses.

Second Notice—In late 2017, over 15,000 world-renowned scientists from 184 countries signed and published a document titled *World Scientists' Warning to Humanity: A Second Notice*. For the second time, the global community of scientists felt it was their fundamental moral duty to warn humanity about catastrophic biodiversity loss and widespread misery for humans. The scientists pleaded for humans to cut greenhouse gas emissions, phase out fossil fuels, reduce deforestation, and reverse the trend of collapsing biodiversity. "Soon it will be too late to shift course away from our failing trajectory, and time is running out," the authors concluded. "We must recognize, in our day-to-day lives and in our governing institutions, that Earth with all its life is our only home."

Generational Threat—"The loss of species, ecosystems and genetic diversity is already a global and generational threat to human well-being. Protecting the invaluable contributions of nature to people will be the defining challenge of decades to come."—Sir Robert Watson, chair of Intergovernmental Science-Policy Platform on Biodiversity and Ecosystem Services (IPBES), a formal scientific association of 132 member governments.

Damaged Food Systems—The way we feed ourselves is the most important social, environmental, health, and economic undertaking of our times. The UN's Intergovernmental Panel on Climate Change (IPCC) issued a report in 2013 that spelled out the trend in blunt language: "[C]limate change will seriously damage the world's ability to feed itself in the coming decades." The report confirmed previous studies' findings that climate change will exacerbate poverty, strain water supplies, make extreme weather more common, and increase conflict around the world. The world's agricultural areas will shift, causing an overall decline in agricultural production. The report pointed out that local food systems are a foundational strategic response to climate chaos. Sustainable agriculture and food systems offer proven models of locally adapted, climate-resilient alternatives that we can build upon to put humanity on a path to a sustainable and resilient food future.

Sixth Extinction—Writer Elizabeth Kolbert won the 2015 Pulitzer Prize for her book *The Sixth Extinction: An Unnatural History*. In her book she reports that over the last half billion years, there have been five mass extinctions, episodes of profound change when the diversity of life on Earth contracted suddenly. Now we are reckoning with the sixth.

Early in the summer of 2018 I heard Kolbert speak in Santa Fe, New Mexico, where she was a guest of the Lannan Foundation. She said the sixth extinction is predicted to be the most devastating global happenstance since an asteroid smashed into Earth some 66 million years ago and wiped out the dinosaurs and hordes of other living creatures.

Kolbert named the five previous extinctions that have occurred on Earth and their causes. Then she talked at length about the sixth extinction currently well underway, an unprecedented biological annihilation that we human beings are wreaking upon our home planet. "This time," Kolbert said, "we are the asteroids."

Our Strongest Lever—The 37 scientists of the EAT-Lancet Commission on Healthy Diets from Sustainable Food Systems in 2019 authored a landmark publication titled *Food in the Anthropocene*. The scientists concluded that food is the single strongest lever to improve human health and environmental sustainability.

Food systems have potential to dramatically increase environmental sustainability and to nurture and improve human health; however, our current food systems are accentuating climate change and fouling ecosystems. Overall the food system is the single largest driver of environmental degradation.

Further, as the commission reported, unhealthy diets now pose a greater risk to morbidity and mortality than unsafe sex and alcohol, drug and tobacco use combined. Thus, an immense challenge facing humanity is to provide a growing world population with healthy diets from sustainable food systems. The commission called for a radical transformation of the global food system.

Oligopoly—Corporations with limited competition, such that competitive pricing does not occur, are called oligopolies. In the realm of food and fiber production, especially in the realm of seeds, the ongoing processes of concentration and vertical integration have established oligopolies. Likewise, oligopolies dominate the various mineral and chemical input enterprises that supply the wherewithal of industrial-scale crop production. In this economic environment, ecosystems are destroyed, formerly independent farmers are driven to become laborers for hire, and thousands of rural residents are forced to abandon the industrialized countryside and move to urban slums, while more and more land comes under remotely managed terms of engagement.

This pattern of metastasizing oligopolies played out dramatically in the United States in the 1970s, '80s, and '90s. The process has been ongoing in the first decades of the 21st century as a result of shakeouts and consolidations. Via this hard-edged business process, human beings have been systematically transformed from independent farmers upon the land into a commodity (labor).

While statistics show that family businesses continue to own the majority of US farmland, more and more of that land is leased out for contract farming. Simultaneously, corporate industrial efficiencies make fewer and fewer units of labor necessary. Thus, unneeded labor units (human beings) are forced to migrate from the countryside to the cities.

In response to this global pattern of expanding oligarchies, Pope Francis authored the 2015 encyclical on the care of our common home, *Laudato Si* (Praise Be). It called attention to the serious and dehumanizing consequences in many places around the world. He wrote, "[F]ollowing the introduction of GMO crops, productive land is concentrated in the hands of a few owners due to the progressive disappearance of small producers, who, as a consequence of the loss of the exploited lands, are obliged to withdraw from direct production." The Pope's encyclical called for broad, responsible scientific and social debate, a debate capable of considering all the available information, and "*calling things by their name.*"

Corporate Colonialism—In a 2018 background report from Food First, executive director Eric Holt-Giménez wrote: "Slavery, exploitation, and dispossession of the land, labor, and products of women, the poor, and people of color are still foundational to the capitalist food system, as are hunger, malnutrition, diet-related disease, and exposure to toxic chemicals. Poor women of color and children, especially girls, bear the brunt of these inequalities."

Deaths of Despair—One of the cultural disasters now unfolding is the significant rise in the number of "deaths of despair," as researchers have come to describe deaths by suicide, alcohol-related liver disease, and drug overdoses. The grim details concerning the increasing numbers of deaths of despair are set out in a report titled *Mortality and Morbidity in the 21st Century* by Professors Angus Deaton and Anne Case.

Ethos—The words *ethos* and *ethics* derive from the Greek root *ethikos*, meaning "moral." The Greek word is the root of our modern English terms for moral competence. While ethics may be individual, ethos is communal and arises out of common experience and insight. Ethos denotes a characteristic spirit—the guiding beliefs and values of a team, a company, a tribe, or a nation. There's an emerging consensus among leading scientists, researchers, and activists that protecting the environment of the Earth is now a matter of life and death. As we confront radically changing circumstances in our economy, energy supply, and food chain, we have an opportunity to change and reconstitute our ethos and the way we live with the land.

Harmony—The UN General Assembly adopted its eighth resolution, "Harmony with Nature" (#71/232), at the winter solstice of 2016. The resolution included this statement: "The significant impact of human activities on the Earth's systems has been widely acknowledged by the UN, the international and scientific community, spiritual leaders, community and indigenous leaders, and leading groups and stakeholders worldwide. Addressing the need to restore our relationship with Nature, and to live in Harmony with Nature, is key to reversing the damage inflicted upon the Earth and protecting it from further detrimental human activity."

Sanity—The right name for the native teaching of the Seventh Generation is sanity. The teaching holds that leaders are responsible for considering the impact of their decisions on the seventh generation of our children yet to come. Back in 1995 I heard the seven generations teaching memorably expounded by Leon Shenandoah, the late elder and chief in service to the Haudenosaunee (Iroquois Six Nations).

Grandfather Leon was standing to speak in a ring of tipis set up for the annual ecumenical Prayer Vigil for the Earth at the base of the Washington Monument in Washington, DC. "Look behind you," he said. "See your sons and your daughters. They are your future. Look farther and see your sons' and your daughters' children and their children's children even unto the Seventh Generation. You have to think of them. That's the way we were taught. Think about it: You yourself are a Seventh Generation. Someone had to think about you."

Chapter 2

Industrial Farms and Food

"To be interested in food but not in food production is clearly absurd."

—Wendell Berry

On the night of September 28, 2012, four former secretaries of the Department of Agriculture (USDA) sat side by side on stage at the Lied Center in Lincoln, Nebraska. They were decked out uniformly in dark suits and ties, ready for a panel on "The Land-Grant Mission of 2012." The panel was part of a weeklong celebration of the 150th anniversary of both the USDA and the Morrill Act that created the land-grant colleges.

John Block held the USDA's top job from 1981 to 1985; the late Clayton Yeutter, from 1989 to 1991; Dan Glickman, from 1995 to 2001; and Mike Johanns, from 2005 to 2007. In turn, they laid out their visions in the context of the evening's subtopic: "Transforming Agriculture for the 2050 World."

Secretary Glickman articulated a catchphrase for the evening, and the other secretaries nodded in agreement. Referencing the iconic film, Glickman said, "If in the 1960s the word for *The Graduate* passing from school into adult life was 'plastics,' then the word for graduates in 2012 and beyond is 'agriculture.' Agriculture is poised to be the dominant industry. It will be necessary to feed two billion more people by 2050."

Jeff Raikes, CEO of the Bill and Melinda Gates Foundation at the time, served as the evening's co-moderator along with UNL's VP for Agriculture and Natural Resources, Ronnie Green. Raikes explained his belief: "We need to see farmers as customers. We need more affordable solutions, and we need to shift the mindset of farmers toward prosperity, somehow enabling them to see farming as a business."

As the evening wore on, the discussion revolved around visions that, as they broke upon my mind, formed an image of global laboratory experiment on nature and on food, a shared conception of genetically modified, chemically enhanced, transnational corporate enterprises engaged in extractive agribusiness.

By the end of the evening I was unmoved, unconvinced, and uninspired about the prospects of the 2050 future they described, a progression of the status quo. We would go forward with food and fiber subsidized, as so many observed have noted, by perpetuating the tragedy of the commons—the despoliation of nature. Having already observed and experienced the consequences of the secretaries' general agricultural vision, as has most of the world, I needed to hear something healthier, a more promising vision of how things could be. I hit the wall hard when John Block took the opportunity on this historic occasion to publicly denigrate sustainable, organic agriculture as "insignificant." He and I see things differently. In point of fact, I see things differently from most of what the panelists shared that evening.

As climate change intensifies, agriculture is invariably becoming an even more critical factor in the world. No doubt. But the secretaries' visions for getting us to 2050 and beyond struck me as describing a material pathway incapable of reckoning with realities far harsher than market forces, and likewise incapable of leading us forward in a healthy, egalitarian manner for the next seven generations.

The impression I took from listening to their visions was that they were encouraging more industrially created, corporately owned genes, the petrochemicals necessary to sustain them in nature, and a continued vertically integrated scale of operation that employs cadres of minimum-wage workers who are being steadily and systematically replaced by machines. That's agri*business* as opposed to agri*culture*. That's not the call of the land. That's not the call of farm and food workers. That's not the call of consumers, and it's not the call of health professionals. Listen closely. The call I hear, distinctly, is a full-throated cry from around the world for fundamental, natural respect for the whole Circle of Life, or Sacred Hoop of Life as it has been spoken of for thousands of years in North America.

Farming as a corporate industrial profit-driven business? Or farming as a way of life in harmony with nature, serving as a clean, healthy, just, and egalitarian foundation for the high-tech digital culture of the present and future, and for the necessary spiritual evolution of humanity?

It's not my intention to dwell overlong on the problems posed by industrial chemical agriculture. But I do need to say something, and to say it emphatically. The problems are too serious, too widespread, too immediate. To ignore or to minimize the problems would constitute dereliction of duty.

Yet my sympathies lie with the farmers who actually work upon the land. A host of commercial factors have constellated to create the present-day, corporately dominated food system. Most farmers, even with the highest of moral intentions, are ultimately cogs in the machine, with their livelihood fully dependent on the status quo structure. This can be changed. This needs to be changed.

My aim is to inform a wide swath of humanity about the problems, and in particular to alert them to the essential opportunities before us to change things for the better. Farmers cannot transform the system by themselves. To maintain our fundamental life supports, and to elevate those supports toward the necessary agroecological ideals, farmers need wide acknowledgment, appreciation, and active support.

We must have large-scale agricultural enterprises and technology to feed the billions of us living together on Earth, but in doing so, we must not sacrifice the health of land, waters, animals, and people for the sake of efficiency and profit. That's squandering our natural wealth. Doing so has led to derangement. It's way past late. Our situation is extreme, and corporate industrial agriculture has been making it more extreme.

The whole gargantuan, super-efficient, chemical-dependent agriborg has been repeatedly whacked upside the head by ugly environmental and human-health realities. Despite the assault of facts, the mega-tentacled complex of agribusiness plows systematically forward into toxic drainage ditches of its own fouling. It is still a way to make a lot of money.

The profit motive in industrial agriculture has over the decades driven us into what Andrew Kimbrell, founder and executive director of the Center for Food Safety, calls "Zombie Agriculture." When I heard him speak at the Mountain West Seed Summit in 2017, Kimbrell said, "This system is already dead. It's a zombie walking. But it's still unbelievably dangerous. It's steadily destroying the planet... Sometimes we look at these dominant forces and wonder, how can we possibly overcome?" Agroecological systems, Kimbrell said, are the future.

This chapter presents an overview of many of the environmental and human health conditions brought about through industrial chemical agriculture. The chapter is an array of facts and consequences, not opinions. Collectively the facts serve to heighten our awareness, and thereby serve as a motivating springboard toward positive solutions for our immediate problems. In the main, those solutions fall under the wide umbrellas of agroecology and deep agroecology.

CONSEQUENCES FOR EARTH

Loss of Topsoil—Many current industrial farming practices contribute to the loss of topsoil, the layer of ground containing most organic matter and the nutrients necessary for plant growth. The US "Federal Strategic Plan for Soil Science" (2016) lays the facts out plainly: "Soil is essential to human life. Not only is it vital for providing most of the world's food, it plays a critical role in ensuring water quality and availability; supports a vast array of non-food products and benefits, including mitigation of climate change; and affects biodiversity important for ecological resilience. These roles make soil essential to modern life."

Topsoil has been eroding faster than it can be replaced, threatening future crop yields. According to the UN's Food and Agriculture Organization (FAO), about a third of the world's topsoil has already been degraded. If soil degradation continues at current rates, we have only about 60 years of farming left.

Extreme Resource Extraction—People have extracted resources from the Earth for millennia, from the first humans who gathered reeds to make a bed or killed an animal for meat to the extraction of oil from below the surface of the Earth. Some of these activities have minimal impact, while some have tremendous, enduring consequences.

Industrial agriculture depends upon mined products used for crop fertilizers and animal feed supplements. Many of those sources are being depleted through systems of extreme resource extraction. For example, the world's main and essential source of phosphorus fertilizer—phosphate rock—took 10 to 15 million years to form from seabeds. Recent studies indicate that phosphorus demand will soon outstrip supply. Along with the well-known phrase *peak oil*, used to describe depletion of that finite resource, there is a parallel phrase, *peak phosphorus,* to describe the decline of mineral fertilizers.

Aquifer Depletion—Roughly 80 percent of water consumption is due to agriculture. This heavy use has led to aquifer depletion and water scarcity in some key agricultural areas. The High Plains Aquifer, found under eight states extending from South Dakota to Texas, is the main water source for one of the world's most productive farming territories. The region is responsible for 20 percent of the country's production of corn, wheat, and cattle. This is also the ranch and farmland that has experienced the most severe declines in groundwater levels

A 2015 study conducted by *USA Today* and *The Desert Sun* took a close look at the problem by examining two decades of measurement data from more than 32,000 wells across the United States. The study found that water levels have declined about 64 percent nationally. The average decline in wells has been more than 10 feet. In some places, the water table dropped more than 100 feet during the two decades of data, or more than five feet per year.

Aquifer Contamination—A 2015 study conducted by researchers at the University of Nebraska–Lincoln (UNL) showed high contamination levels of uranium in both the Great Plains and California's Central Valley Aquifers. The toxic uranium is released in the aquifers through interaction with nitrates—a common groundwater contaminant that originates mainly from chemical fertilizers spread on fields and mass quantities of manure from industrial-scale animal confinement operations (CAFOs).

Surface Water Pollution—Applying too much fertilizer, whether manure or synthetic fertilizer, or applying fertilizer at the wrong time can pollute nearby waterbodies with nitrogen and phosphorus. The Environmental Protection Agency (EPA) has repeatedly identified agriculture as the industry with the largest negative impact on water quality in US rivers and lakes.

Dead Zones—As currently practiced, industrial agriculture allows copious volumes of chemical fertilizers and pesticides to run off into streams and rivers, and eventually into the ocean. Meanwhile, scientific measurements show emphatically that global warming is taking place 10 to 100 times faster than in recent geological history. This combination of circumstances has created conditions that have spawned over 400 dead zones in oceans around the world—vast suffocating spaces devoid of oxygen where no sea life can exist. These putrid regions suffocate shrimp, fish, and hundreds of other sea creatures. Year after year, these nightmarish, fouled regions of the seas continue to metastasize and to breed death. The largest as of 2018 was in the Gulf of Oman, measuring 63,700 square miles—as big as the state of Florida. The lifeless ocean territory in the Gulf of Mexico was said to have grown as large as the state of Rhode Island.

Frying the Planet—The University of Minnesota published a blockbuster study in 2017 in the *Proceedings of the National Academy of Sciences.* The study reported that our foremost industrial corn production systems are frying the planet with the release of nitrous oxide, a compound that traps far more heat in our atmosphere than carbon dioxide does, thereby upping average temperatures. Data show that industrial corn production is a critical factor in climate change.

According to the UN's Intergovernmental Panel on Climate Change (IPCC), agriculture in general is responsible for a huge detrimental impact on climate change. Agriculture has, in fact, contributed nearly as much to climate change as deforestation. Improper soil management, methane emissions from cattle, and the production and combustion of biofuels are all sources of agricultural greenhouse gas emissions. The existing global food system is estimated to contribute one-third of total emissions of greenhouse gasses linked to global warming.

Insect Armageddon—There is alarming evidence that insect populations worldwide are in rapid decline. Professor Dave Goulson of the University of Sussex, a coauthor of a comprehensive insect study, told *The New York Times* in October 2017 that we are "on course for ecological Armageddon.... If we lose the insects, then everything is going to collapse." His study, which tracked flying insects collected in nature, found that in just 25 years, the total biomass of these insects declined by an astonishing 76 percent. The reasons for the decline are not entirely clear, but scientists suspect two main culprits: the use of pesticides and a lack of habitat.

The world's insects are speeding down the path to extinction, threatening a consequent "catastrophic collapse of nature's ecosystems," according to the first global scientific review published in the peer-reviewed journal *Biological Conservation*. One devastating impact of insect loss is on the many birds, reptiles, amphibians, and fish that eat insects. Without this food source, all these animals starve. The main drivers of the insect decline are habitat loss by conversion to intensive agriculture, pesticides, other agrochemicals, invasive species, and climate change.

Animal Anguish—The confined animal feeding operations (CAFOs) that industrialize the lives of billions of cows, pigs, chickens, and other animals eaten by human beings create deplorable life circumstances for them. In the US there are well over 10,000 CAFOs producing beef, pork, poultry, eggs, dairy products, and other animal-based foods.

Animals feel what is happening to them. They are inescapably aware of the cramped, crowded, stinking circumstances in which they dwell. Like human beings, farm animals have neuroanatomical structures and pathways that are key to feelings. Thus, there is a scientific as well as a common-sense basis for appreciating the reality that animals have feelings and emotional lives.

How does this translate in terms of the relationship human beings have, no matter how remote, with the animals they eat? What happens when animals—and the flesh that constitutes their bodies—are permeated with the feelings of misery engendered by living in CAFO conditions? Does the distress of a creature raised in a CAFO creature translate into their meat and then subtly into human flesh and emotional state?

As well as industrializing the lives of animals, and inflicting untold suffering upon them, CAFOs impose burdensome costs on taxpayers and their communities. Those taxpayer costs include water and air pollution, lower property values, and government subsidies to the corporations paid out of public tax dollars. CAFOs generate vast, polluting quantities of animal waste and foul, permeating odors that sour the atmosphere for miles. All of these ancillary costs are largely unaccounted for when these kinds of projects are proposed. The UN's Food and Agriculture Organization estimates that of all troublesome greenhouse emissions, farmed animals, cattle in particular, contribute a whopping 14.5 percent.

Consolidation—In recent years big farms have gotten bigger and absorbed smaller farms further and further into consolidated industrial business enterprises. By and large, the growth of these farms has come as they have acquired small- and mid-sized farms that could not compete financially. According to a 2018 USDA report, *Three Decades of Consolidation in U.S. Agriculture*, "consolidation of acreage and production has been persistent, widespread, and pronounced in crop production."

Vertical integration is a business arrangement in which the company selling a product, whether that product is a widget or a frozen dinner, owns and commands the supply chain, all the way back to the mine, or the farm, that was the source of the raw material for the final product. Agriculture is undergoing a process of vertical integration with allied industries, usually through contract farming. The economic pressure coming from multinational corporations on down to the human-scale farm is hyper-intense: get big or get steamrolled.

Undermining—According to a comprehensive UN study of the plants, animals, and micro-organisms that help to put food on our tables, the capacity of the world to produce food is being undermined by our failure to protect biodiversity.

The UN's Food and Agriculture Organization's Commission on Genetic Resources for Food and Agriculture reported in 2019 that scientists have found evidence that the natural support systems underpinning the human diet are deteriorating around the world. This deterioration intensifies as farms, cities, and factories gobble up land and pump out chemicals. Approximately 20 percent of the Earth's vegetated surface has become less productive over the last 20 years.

The UN report noted a debilitating loss of soil biodiversity, forests, grasslands, coral reefs, mangroves, seagrass beds, and genetic diversity in crop and animal species. In the oceans, as much as one-third of key fishing areas has been overharvested.

Transition—The idea that pesticides are essential to feed a fast-growing global population is a myth, according to UN food and pollution experts. A report presented to the UN Human Rights Council in March 2017 severely criticized global corporations that manufacture pesticides, accusing them of aggressive, unethical marketing tactics, heavy lobbying of governments to obstruct reforms and paralyze global pesticide restrictions, and systematic denial of harms.

The report said pesticides have "catastrophic impacts on the environment, human health and society as a whole," including an estimated 200,000 deaths a year from acute poisoning. Its authors concluded: "It is time to create a global process to transition toward safer and healthier food and agricultural production."

CONSEQUENCES FOR PEOPLE

Overweight and Undernourished—A 2017 *New York Times* examination of corporate records, epidemiological studies, and government reports—as well as interviews with scores of nutritionists and health experts around the world—revealed a sea change in the way food is produced, distributed, and advertised across much of the globe. The shift is contributing to a new epidemic of diabetes and heart disease, also chronic illnesses that are fed by soaring rates of obesity. Around the world, more people are now obese than underweight. Scientists say the growing availability of high-calorie, nutrient-poor foods is generating a new type of malnutrition, one in which a growing number of people are both overweight and undernourished.

Food and agriculture reporter Helena Bottemiller Evich noted in a 2017 *Politico* article, "In agricultural research it's been understood for some time that many of our most important foods have been getting less nutritious. Measurements of fruits and vegetables show that their minerals, vitamin, and protein content has dropped measurably over the past 50 to 70 years."

Epidemic Obesity—More than one-third of the US population is obese, a proportion that has increased by 65 percent over the last 30 years. This increased prevalence of obesity, and the related risk of diabetes, heart disease, stroke, and other diseases, is tied to overconsumption of some of the main products of industrial agriculture, such as sugars and highly processed foods. Global obesity rates are on the rise, and the number of children and adolescents with obesity has increased more than tenfold over the past four decades, according to a study published in *The Lancet* in October 2017.

Dietary Impacts—A 2018 report from PIRG Education Fund and the Frontier Group, *Reaping What We Sow: How the Practices of Industrial Agriculture Put Our Health and Environment at Risk*, sets out the case plainly: "Shaped by modern technologies, financial influences and public policy, American agriculture has evolved into an efficient system that produces all the food the country needs and more. However, in addition to the benefits that our food system offers, the shift to larger and more specialized farms has damaged public health and the environment." Diabetes, heart disease, many cancers, many allergies, and many other modern diseases have their origins in the modern diet of processed food, which arises from processed, chemicalized soil.

Inflamed Guts—It's difficult to escape television advertisements for patent medicines claiming to be *the cure* for ailments such as Crohn's Disease, constipation, diabetes, gas, bloating, Irritable Bowel Syndrome (IBS), and even—heaven help us—Inflamed Bowel Syndrome. The ads invariably hawk drugs to treat your irate bowel, though the medications themselves come with a laundry list of potential side effects such as fatigue, vomiting, constipation, bloating, incontinence, upper respiratory infection, even death.

The use of antibiotics in human and farm-animal populations increased rampantly over past decades as factory farms proliferated. In the same window of time, sales also increased for probiotics and prebiotics in consumer efforts to sooth their rebellious guts. Thus, through pharmaceuticals, our human innards have morphed into a biotic battleground. Studies estimate the prevalence of IBS at 10 to 25 percent of the population.

Depression—Diets high in processed foods lead to a higher rate of depression, a condition also known as Major Depressive Disorder (MDD), according to a 2018 study published in the journal *Molecular Psychiatry*. About the study, principal author Dr. Camille Lassale of University

College London said: "There is compelling evidence to show that there is a relationship between the quality of your diet and your mental health.... There is also emerging evidence that shows that the relationship between the gut and brain plays a key role in mental health and that this axis is modulated by gastrointestinal bacteria, which can be modified by our diet." Based on data from 41 studies, her research team advised that dietary advice should inform mental health treatment.

Your Choice—Each individual holds primary responsibility for his or her own health. Thus, it's important to note that, according to the Centers for Disease Control and Prevention, only one in ten Americans eats the daily recommended quantities of fruits and vegetables. Meanwhile, a majority of Americans regularly choose to eat the kinds of highly processed foods that are known to cause illnesses over the long term. Processed, chemicalized industrial food sickens people in a variety of ways.

In an October 2017 report from the International Panel of Experts on Sustainable Food Systems (IPES-Food), lead author Cecilia Rocha wrote: "Food systems are making us sick. Unhealthy diets are the most obvious link but are only one of many pathways through which food and farming systems affect human health." The study found that many of the most severe health conditions afflicting populations around the world, from respiratory diseases to a range of cancers and systemic livelihood stresses, are linked to industrial food and farming practices. They specifically referenced chemical-intensive agriculture, concentrated production, the mass production and marketing of ultra-processed foods, and global supply chains with few regulations or safeguards.

Processed Cancers—One lifestyle factor more than any other accounts for your likelihood of developing cancer. A 2018 study of French adults revealed that people who consume more processed food are much more likely to develop all kinds of cancers. Most of the ultra-processed products were sugar-rich beverages and foods. The research finding held true for every category of participants in the study: men and women, young and old, smokers and nonsmokers, exercisers and nonexercisers. Acknowledging that cancer represents a major worldwide burden, the researchers wrote: "Therefore, reaching a balanced and diversified diet (along with avoidance of tobacco use and reduction in alcohol intake) should be considered one of the most important modifiable risk factors in the primary prevention of cancer."

Staggering Health Costs—The industrial food system is mostly to blame for staggering health-care costs, according to *Unravelling the Food-Health Nexus*, a 2018 report from the International Panel of Experts on Sustainable

Food Systems (IPES-Food) and the Global Alliance for the Future of Food. Their study documented the reality that food systems affect health through multiple, interconnected pathways, generating severe human and economic costs. While the industrial food and farming model does not bear the entire burden for these problems, it has failed to provide a recipe for addressing them individually or collectively. According to the report, the impacts are interconnected, self-reinforcing, complex, widespread, and severe. The report argues strongly for reforming food and farming systems on the fundamental grounds of protecting human health.

Cavalcade of Chemicals—Heavy pesticide use harms people and the environment. Some of the most commonly used pesticides in the US have been linked to cancer, autism spectrum disorders, and lower IQ. Farmworkers and their families face heightened risk. The overuse of herbicides has created herbicide-resistant weeds, which have infected 60 million acres of crops and will make future farming more difficult.

The US Centers for Disease Control and Prevention reports that there are traces of 29 different pesticides in the body of an average American. Overall, that agglomeration of synthetic chemicals increases risk for birth defects, diminished IQ, cancer, depression, and diseases such as Alzheimer's and Parkinson's. Safety limits for food don't account for how different pesticides mix together, accumulate in the body, and interact. Together they create a "cocktail effect"—a mixture of the multitude of synthetic chemicals with a greater likelihood of being harmful than single, isolated chemicals.

Poisoned Farmworkers—Hilal Elver, the UN Special Rapporteur on the Right to Food, reported in 2017 that while consumers in developed countries are usually protected from pesticides, farmworkers often are not. In the US, 90 percent of farmworkers are undocumented; their consequent lack of legal protections and health insurance puts them at high risk from pesticide use. As the special rapporteur noted, "[C]hronic exposure to pesticides has been linked to cancer, Alzheimer's and Parkinson's diseases, hormone disruption, developmental disorders and sterility."

Pesticides and Food Insecurity—A 2017 report from the UN's International Panel of Experts on Sustainable Food Systems (IPES-Food) blames pesticides for food insecurity. For much of the past century, the panel reports, chemical companies have told consumers that pesticides are essential for keeping crop yields high, which they argue is necessary for feeding the world's growing population. Chemicals have been helpful, but their use has come at a steep cost that, the sustainable experts posited, no longer outweighs the drawbacks and problems. In the report, the panel takes a strong stance against the use of industrial agrochemicals, declaring that in fact they are not necessary for feeding the world. The report argues that it's time to overturn the myth that pesticides can feed the world and come up with better, safer ways of producing our food.

Additive Eruption—Americans are consuming a wholesale eruption of food additives. In the 1950s there were only about 800 food additives. Today there are more than 10,000, many of them dubious and provoking a cascade of health complaints. Since the days of the George H. W. Bush administration, 1989–1993, the US Food and Drug Administration (FDA) has shrugged its regulatory shoulders. It provides no scrutiny of food additives to determine whether they are safe for human consumption. The government allows corporations to monitor themselves. Over 275 chemicals used by 56 companies appear to be marketed as GRAS (Generally Recognized as Safe) and are used in many products based on companies' safety determinations that, pursuant to current regulations, do not need to be reported to the FDA or the public. This is likely the tip of an ugly iceberg.

Declining Sperm Counts—For years, scientists have warned that male sperm counts are dropping around the world. As published in the journal *Human Reproduction Update*, the largest, most rigorous study to date shows sperm counts are down by nearly 60 percent in North America, Europe, New Zealand, and Australia, while over the last 40 years, sperm concentration has dropped by 52 percent overall. These data reveal a significant and continuing decline in male reproductive health.

According to Dr. Shanna Swan, lead author of the 2017 report, farm chemical and phthalates (chemicals that leach into food through plastic) are major contributors to the problem. Smoking, obesity, and lack of exercise are also factors. "Men who have lower sperm count or men who are infertile go on to die earlier," Swan reported, citing higher rates of cardiovascular disease, diabetes, and testicular cancer for men with lower sperm counts.

Colon Cancer—More young people are dying of colon cancer. As reported by *The New York Times* in the summer of 2017, colorectal cancer rates are rising in people in their 20s and 30s. Younger Americans aren't just getting cancer diagnoses earlier, they are dying of colorectal cancer at slightly higher rates than in previous decades. In May 2018 the American Cancer Society for the first time recommended that people initiate colorectal cancer screening at age 45 instead of waiting until age 50. The new guidelines sent a clear message that colorectal cancer is no longer a disease of just older people. Researchers say no one really knows why colon cancer is occurring more commonly in young people, but since the function of the colon is to process the food we eat, it is logical to recognize that food is a likely factor, if not the primary cause.

Cultural Erosion—In a landmark report issued in October 2017, the UN's IPES-Food panel made a powerful statement that garnered scant attention in global media: "Good food is a cornerstone of good health, and this fundamental relationship is widely understood," the researchers wrote. "Yet profound changes in global food systems over the last decades have resulted in significant negative impacts on health and well-being that range from food insecurity to chronic disease, and from environmental degradation to diminished economic opportunity and the erosion of culture. These impacts are experienced unequally across the globe and between different groups of people in different places."

The IPES-Food report continued: "Mergers are increasingly allowing firms to control information flows along the chain and exercise huge power over the trajectory of food systems." As the "get big" impulse reverberated across the land, it eviscerated communities—social structures that were once vibrant. It destroyed ways of life.

Nanotechnology—The invisible micro-mechanistic food interventions being advanced by industry are now incarnate via nanotechnology. That's the practice of manipulating materials on an atomic or molecular scale, then incorporating the synthetic molecules into processed stuff, including our food. The scale of nanotech is so infinitesimal that it's a mind stretch for most people. A sheet of newspaper, for example, is about 100,000 nanometers thick.

The chemical-food industry has already incorporated nanomaterials into dietary supplements as well as packaging materials and cutting boards. The industry claims that their nano-products make food safer, and they have dozens of direct food applications in development. Corporations are churning out a complex mishmash of novel, synthetic materials to impact the industrial food chain, and eventually our bodies and souls. They are doing it with minimal or no regulation. Consider: Unbeknownst to consumers, the market offers more than 300 foods and food packaging materials that likely contain engineered nanomaterials, according to the Center for Food Safety.

Rising Suicide Rate—Farmers, farmworkers, and food workers face a range of severe occupational health risks, from pesticide poisoning to stress-driven mental health impacts. A 2012 study by the Centers for Disease Control and Prevention found that people working in agriculture—including farmers, farm laborers, ranchers, fishers, and lumber harvesters—take their lives at a rate higher than any other occupation.

The data suggested the suicide rate for agricultural workers in 17 states was nearly five times higher compared with the rate for the general population. Those statistics continue to climb. The US farmer suicide crisis echoes a much larger suicide crisis happening globally. The CDC report suggested that possible causes for the high suicide rate among farmers include "social isolation, potential for financial losses, barriers to and unwillingness to seek mental health services, and access to lethal means."

Global Food System Broken—A coalition of 130 national academies of science and medicine, the InterAcademy Partnership (IAP), declared in 2018 that the global food system is broken. The system requires a radical overhaul not just in farming practices but also in consumption patterns. According to the IAP, the global food system is responsible for a third of all greenhouse gas emissions, which is more than all emissions from transport, heating, lighting, and air conditioning combined. The resulting global warming is now damaging food production through extreme weather events such as floods and droughts.

According to one of the report's authors, Tim Benton of the University of Leeds in the UK, "Whether you look at it from a human health, environmental or climate perspective, our food system is currently unsustainable and given the challenges that will come from a rising global population that is a really [serious] thing to say."

Global Syndemic—Just weeks after the British medical journal *The Lancet* released its landmark *Food in the Anthropocene* report, cited in chapter 1, it published a second report from a separate commission: *The Global Syndemic of Obesity, Undernutrition and Climate Change: The Lancet Commission Report*. That commission involved 26 experts from 14 countries.

In the report the commission wrote that humanity is actively under threat from three global pandemics, all of them directly linked to the way we eat. Those pandemics are undernutrition, obesity, and climate change. All are serious threats for human beings. Their interactions create a hazardous impact greater than merely one or even two afflictions.

In combination, the three pandemics establish a global *syndemic*. That's a set of linked health problems involving two or more afflictions that interact synergistically to drive conditions into a danger zone. The commission found that pandemics of malnutrition and obesity interact with climate change in a feedback loop. Together they represent an existential threat to humans and the planet. In conclusion, the commission noted that the evidence is now overwhelming that diet is the largest cause of climate change and biodiversity loss.

Go Agroecological or Go Extinct—As this chapter comes to a close, I'm inspired to mention a fifth USDA secretary: Earl Butz, who served from 1971 to 1976. Mr. Butz died in 2008, but his mantra lives on. His policies favored large-scale enterprises and dramatically diminished support for family farms. His philosophy and his government policies were encapsulated in the infamous phrase he directed at farmers: "Get big or get out." Butz's *get-big* message was a death knell for millions of farm families who once populated rural America. The trajectory to consolidation, vertical integration, and central corporate control and colonization has continued unchecked in the ensuing decades.

These realities underscore the critical importance of the resilient, community farm and food initiatives that have arisen so dynamically in the US and abroad over the last 40 years or more. The emerging, networked community food movement, with its emphasis on organic, sustainable, agroecological farming systems imbued with economic and social justice, arises in a time of vast environmental contamination. Agriculture can be transformed from being the major contributor to pollution and climate change, as it is today, to being a major remedy for these serious troubles. That's what agroecology and deep agroecology are all about.

Based on the hard realities in the realm of industrial-chemical agriculture, it's time to uproot Earl Butz's infamous "Get big or get out" farm motto and to supplant it with something both wise and realistic: "Go agroecological or go extinct."

Chapter 3

Elements of Agroecology

"Agroecology is the future of farming, and its principles cannot be practiced soon enough. Agroecology is a major global force or movement that's going to be gaining recognition and increasing credibility."

—John Ikerd

As I have come to appreciate while learning about agroecology, the subject has depth, breadth, and sophistication. Agroecology offers a penetrating critique of the status quo, and a far-reaching, environmentally enlightened, justice-based vision of better ways to care for land, plants, animals, and people.

Rather than a mechanistic formula for domination of nature to produce profits for a small group of investors, the core ideas of agroecology arise naturally from living, rhythmic, biological appreciation of the world and the life that inhabits the world. Consequently, the global movement toward agroecology has the capacity to recognize and to employ systems that bring human needs into right relation with the needs of the natural world.

As University of Nebraska–Lincoln Professor Chuck Francis noted in *Agroecology: The Ecology of Food Systems*, food systems are vast and fragile and exist in the multiple and interacting matrices of our increasingly complex national and global cultures. Agroecology recognizes farms as ecosystems embedded in broader landscapes and social settings, with which they interact continually and significantly. In the book's introduction, Francis writes, "We define agroecology as the integrative study of the ecology of the entire food system, encompassing ecological, economic, and social dimensions."

For a while the term *agroecology* simply defined the application of ecology in agriculture—a meaning that is still used. But starting in the 1960s, Francis notes, the concept broadened. Increasing awareness among farmers, academics, and the general public about how humans manage the landscape for food, and the consequences of those management practices, set the stage for the necessary evolution of agroecology.

While agroecological pathways can be traced to the evolutionary symbiosis of agronomy and ecology, other disciplines such as botany, zoology, sociology, anthropology, ethics, economics, and native wisdom ways are by now also part of the whole. In consilience (or convergence) these disciplines provide a range of insight-yielding vantage points for studying the food system, for developing a broader set of criteria for evaluation beyond monetary profitability, and for transforming the farm and food system in a manifestly healthy way.

In 2018 Dartmouth College's Environmental Studies program published a job notice for an assistant professor of agroecology, tenure track. The list of qualifications for applicants gives a picture of how sophisticated the field has become. "The successful candidate will have a strong foundation in ecological science and its applications in the area of sustainable agriculture. In addition, the ideal candidate will take an interdisciplinary approach that engages with the social, economic, and governance dimensions of food systems. We seek a colleague whose research and classroom teaching employ field- and lab-based methods to examine topics such as the role of ecological practices in improving soil health, reducing greenhouse gas emissions, and conserving biodiversity; the development of integrated food and energy systems; and the landscape-scale interactions of farming with forest and watershed conservation."

What follows is an overview of agroecology as it originated, and as it is developing.

HISTORY

Many basic agroecological methods have been practiced in the Americas and elsewhere around the world for centuries under a variety of cultural impulses, and with varying degrees of success. However, it was not until 1928 that the term *agroecology* was used to designate the combination of agronomy and ecology. The term was coined by Basil M. Bensin, a Russian-born scholar who immigrated to the US and wound up working as an agronomist for the Alaska Agricultural Experiment Station. He suggested using "agroecology" to describe the use of ecological methods in research on commercial crops. Thus, the word agroecology entered general usage in roughly the same time period as the terms *organic* and *biodynamic*.

In the near century since the word was first articulated, the definition and scope of agroecology have evolved to encompass a broad vision and also a formal study of the role of agriculture in the world. For academics, agroecology established an interdisciplinary framework with which to examine the activity of agriculture not as an isolated activity but as part of an ecology: a matrix of environmental, economic, social, and cultural dimensions. During the 1970s, the term agroecology gradually emerged to designate a movement. This broader perspective encouraged closer relationships with farmer organizations, consumer-citizen groups, and social movements.

Professor Efraím Hernández Xolocotzi, who researched indigenous systems of knowledge in Mexico, observed that modern agricultural systems lost their ecological foundation when economic factors became the primary driving force in the food system. He developed influential education programs in agroecology. Food production as a profit-making business or as a way of life?

In 1982, in a seminal article, "Agroecologia del Tropico Americano," Patricio Montaldo (1927–2016), professor of agricultural sciences at the University of Chile at the time, developed the insight further. He argued that when designing and implementing agricultural systems, the socio-economic context cannot be separated. Personal and community life, and economic well-being, are linked to farming and food production at every level.

"Agroecology is deeply rooted in the ecological rationale of traditional small-scale agriculture," wrote Professor Miguel A. Altieri in his essay "What is Agroecology?" He wrote that complex traditional knowledge systems are the root of long-established, successful agricultural systems. Those systems are characterized by diversity of domesticated crop and animal species, maintained and enhanced by indigenous soil, water, and biodiversity management regimes. Altieri is an agronomist and entomologist at the University of California–Berkeley. His research helped launch agroecology as an academic discipline. According to his writings, there are some 350 million peasant farms around the world that feed about half of the global population using traditional means and methods. Many of those farms optimize their systems with agroecological approaches that are both biodiverse and resilient.

The relationship between agronomists and native agrarians, often subsistence farmers, has been characterized as an exchange of wisdoms. These developing relationships are built on a recognition and acknowledgment that while science is an important way of discovering and knowing, local, indigenous knowledge approaches and systems—developed over thousands of years—are also essential and beneficial. Together they create a whole. This dimension of agroecology—the multifaceted matrix of relationships among farms, plants, animals, food, and people—is what I seek to highlight in writing about deep agroecology.

There is a realization emerging in some precincts of the scientific community, a realization that indigenous cultures have as part of their core philosophy for hundreds if not thousands of years understood, that everything you do has an effect on everything else. Everything is interconnected. In farming you are working with life and life processes, and they are complex and unique, so all actions become important.

The development of agroecology varies from country to country, with the movement well established in some nations, while other nations are just waking up to the necessity and potential. Agroecology is most developed in countries with a deep local and traditional agrarian culture, such as Spain and Mexico. Thanks to strong social movements, other nations are also well advanced in agroecology.

ELEMENTS

In a time of tumultuous transition, agroecology is a leading idea, a stabilizing and improving idea composed of many elements. To serve as a primer on the visions and methods that constitute the field of agroecology, I offer up the following introductory list, appreciating that there are other elements practitioners and scholars would likely add.

A Way of Life—Agroecology espouses a way of life in dialogue with life through the language of nature rather than a profit-driven business model. It is not a rigid set of technologies or production practices but rather an approach based on principles that can be practiced in different ways in different places, with integral contributions from local reality and culture. Agroecology espouses a way of life rather than a marketing angle.

Intertwined—The UN's Food and Agriculture Organization (FAO) has declared that the world must change from radically polluting, petroleum-based industrial agricultural practices to sustainable systems. Agroecologists recognize these multiple crises in the realms of water, soil degradation, climate chaos, and public health epidemics associated with pesticides, as well as from chemicalized and processed foods. Agroecology also recognizes that global environmental and social problems are intertwined.

Common Sense—The precautionary principle is a simple, common-sense ethical guideline that is part of ecology and agroecology, but which is so fundamental to sustainability that it is worth reaffirming. The precautionary principle holds that if an action or policy has a suspected risk of causing harm to the public or to the environment, the burden of proof that it is not harmful falls on those promoting the product or the action. In other words, you must establish that your action or product will not cause harm before you promulgate it and actually cause harm to human beings or to the natural world essential to life. The precautionary principle is a statutory requirement in the law of the European Union but has no legal standing in the United States. The US has, in fact, lobbied actively and secretly—without citizen knowledge or approval—to pressure European governments to ease or overlook the precautionary principle in various cases.

Health—A fundamental tenet of agroecology is the idea that agriculture should sustain and enhance the health of soil, plants, animals, and human beings. Part of this enhancement, it's understood, is the concept that agroecosystems should mimic the biodiversity levels and functioning of natural ecosystems. Experience has demonstrated that this cooperative approach sustains and enhances life. Agroecology is based on living ecological systems and cycles, and the science of agroecology has made great strides forward in understanding the critical ecology of farm systems, as well as the tools and techniques that make such a system workable and sustainable.

Clean food also, naturally, makes a tremendous difference in human health. A comprehensive French study that followed 70,000 adults over the course of five years yielded convincing evidence in 2018. The researchers reported that their study found that people who ate organic food most frequently had 25 percent fewer cancers overall than people who never ate organic.

Fairness—Agroecology is a set of principles rather than hard-and-fast procedures. The spirit of the movement is built on relationships that require fairness in business dealings, employment arrangements, and with high regard for the common environment. Food co-ops and CSA farms are just two of the many initiatives that strive toward this agroecological ideal.

Diversity—Rather than vast monocultures (sprawling farmland given over to growing a single, homogenous crop, such as corn or soybeans), agroecology recognizes the essential biological value of diversity. To support diversity agroecologists follow practices such as mixed cropping, intercropping, perennial cropping, agroforestry, and integration of farm animals into the ecosystem. These practices amplify the positive effects of biodiversity on productivity through better use of sunlight, water, soil resources, and the strategic regulation of pest populations.

Transition—Agroecology seeks to transform industrial agriculture by transitioning food systems away from polluting, fossil fuel–based production for export crops and biofuels. The general consensus is to cultivate an alternative agricultural paradigm that encourages local and national food production by small and family farmers and that is based on local innovation, resources, and solar energy. Large-scale agricultural initiatives that are clean, sustainable, and just have a role in agroecology, as I understand it, but with social, cultural, and environmental concerns sharing the leading values. Authority and power are established in association rather than in hierarchy.

Food Sovereignty—La Via Campesina, an umbrella organization that connects many local farmer groups and movements, began in 1993 when farmer representatives from Latin America and four continents—transnation-al peasants, as they identify themselves—convened for a conference. From that beginning, La Via Campesina ("the way of the farmer") came to represent 200 million farm-ers in 73 countries all over the world.

At the World Food Summit in 1996, the organiza-tion defined a key term: "Food sovereignty is the right of peoples to healthy and culturally appropriate food pro-duced through sustainable methods and their right to de-fine their own food and agriculture systems. It develops a model of small-scale sustainable production benefiting communities and their environment.

"Food sovereignty prioritizes local food production and consumption, giving a country the right to protect its local producers from cheap imports and to control its production. It includes the struggle for land and genuine agrarian reform that ensures that the rights to use and manage lands, territories, water, seeds, farm animals, and biodiversity are in the hands of those who produce food and not of the corporate sector."

Food sovereignty was recognized as a pathway toward revitalizing indigenous food systems and practices and for actively engaging traditional and emerging ecological knowledge. The movement became central to indigenous peoples' mobilization for self-determination in the Amer-icas as well as globally.

Local Systems—Under the ideals of food sovereignty, food is first of all appreciated as essential sustenance for human beings and the communities to which they belong. Only secondarily is food regarded and treated as a commodity to be traded. Local and regional provision takes precedence over supplying distant markets. The "free trade" policies that prevent developing countries from protecting their own agriculture—for example, through subsidies and tariffs—are regarded as inimical to food sovereignty. Food sovereignty places control over territory, land, grazing, water, seeds, farm animals, and fish populations on local food providers and respects their rights. They can use and share them in socially and environmentally sustainable ways that conserve diversity.

Particulars of Place—Agroecology holds a fundamental appreciation of the reality that every farm and every farmer is different. Design of individual farms using principles of ecology is expanded to the levels of landscape, community, and bioregion, with emphasis on uniqueness of place, people, and the other life forms that inhabit that area. Agroecological approaches are based on understanding and managing ecological processes and biological functions to increase and sustain crop and farmed animal productivity, to efficiently recycle inputs, and to build soil fertility, while minimizing harmful impacts on soil, air, water, wildlife, and human health.

Food for People—The right to food that's healthy and culturally appropriate is a basic legal demand underpinning food sovereignty. Guaranteeing this right requires policies that support diversified food production. Food is not regarded as primarily a commodity to be traded or speculated on for profit but rather as sustenance for human beings.

Social Process—In his 2016 essay "Toward a People's Agroecology," Blain Snipstal, a member of the Black Dirt Farm Collective in Maryland, wrote, "Agroecology is a tool for social struggle—that is, to use it to fundamentally change the relations of power in the food system and as a way for healing of our Mother Earth, at local and national levels. It is not just a mere form of Sustainable Agriculture…. Agroecology is a political and social methodology and process, as much as it is an ecological alternative to agribusiness."

Right to Live and Work with Dignity—Through the principles of food sovereignty, agroecology asserts the right of food providers to live and work in dignity. Many small farmers suffer violence, marginalization, and racism from corporate landowners and governments. People are often pushed off their land by agribusiness or mining concerns, and agricultural workers can face severe exploitation and in some cases be impressed into bonded labor.

Women—Around the world women represent the core strength and cohesiveness of the rural economy, especially in developing countries. Women are half of the world's farmers, yet their role and knowledge are often ignored and their rights are violated. Agroecology explicitly acknowledges and honors the role of women in farming the Earth and feeding the people of the Earth. Women's knowledge, values, vision, and leadership are appreciated as being critical for moving forward. Agroecology offers women equality and the enhanced status they are due as the majority of farmers active in the world. For agroecology to achieve its full potential, there must be fair distribution of power, tasks, decision making, and remuneration. Agroecology recognizes this explicitly and actively promotes respect for and empowerment of women.

Farmer to Farmer—A key component of the agroecological method used to achieve food sovereignty is termed *campesino-a-campesino*, PtP (peasant to peasant), or farmer-to-farmer knowledge exchange, which is a way to strengthen social relations within and between communities. The people themselves are the main players in generating and sharing knowledge and technology. Similarly, the collaboration between researchers from universities and farmer research projects allows farmers to have greater social standing than in the milieu of industrial agriculture, where they are valued primarily for their labor and simply told what to do. Farmer-to-farmer exchanges have proven themselves.

Capable—The International Assessment of Agricultural Knowledge, Science and Technology for Development (IAASTD) was a high-level study initiated by the World Bank in 2002. After studying the global farm and food matrix intensively, the IAASTD concluded that small-scale systems of agroecology are capable of producing enough food for the developing world while helping to preserve and replenish natural resources.

A 2017 report published by the United Nations Special Rapporteur on the Right to Food came to similar conclusions, arguing that more sustainable systems could double food production in certain regions. According to the FAO, right now about 70 percent of the world's food is produced by smallholder farmers, and they produce that food on only 25 percent of the world's arable land.

Soil Fertility—Healthy, living soil, rich in vibrant microbial life, gives rise to strong, healthy plants, which give rise to strong, healthy animals, people, and the overall ecosystem. Organic soil sequesters carbon, and thus has a direct impact of mitigating climate change. Agroecology embraces this reality and has a track record of meeting farming challenges in a cost-effective manner. Research has found that applying agroecological methods can result in high yields for each crop in a rotation sequence. Long-term studies have found that organic practices—a specific set of agroecological practices that eschew the use of harmful synthetic chemical inputs—typically improve soil health and also demonstrate that economic returns for organic crops can be greater than for conventional crops, despite higher labor costs.

Climate Stabilizing—As outlined by senior climate scientist James Hansen in his paper "Young People's Burden," in addition to keeping fossil fuels in the ground, we also need to remove excess CO_2 from the air. Anything less is a prescription for disaster. Agroecology, with its particular capacities, is in a strong position to contribute significantly to stabilizing global climate changes. While industrial-chemical agriculture exacerbates climate change, agroecological approaches sequester carbon and thereby help stabilize the climate. When designed and managed with agroecological principles, farming systems exhibit diversity, productivity, resilience, and efficiency. They strengthen the "immune system" of agricultural systems by enhancing healthy biodiversity, a.k.a. "life."

Native Knowledge—In "Peasant Agroecology for Food Sovereignty and Mother Earth," a study booklet from La Via Campesina, the association proclaims: "We believe that the origin of agroecology lies in the accumulated knowledge and knowhow of rural peoples, systematized by a dialogue between different types of knowledge (*diálogo de saberes*) in order to produce the 'science,' the movement, and the practice of agroecology."

Learning, sharing, and social cohesion are at the heart of agroecology. These social dynamics create opportunities for uniting and mobilizing. Whereas native peoples and ways have historically been considered irrelevant by most agronomists and mainstream development experts, agroecology respects and integrates into praxis a range of local indigenous customs and knowledge and tradition. La Via Campesina has been deepened and strengthened by *un diálogo de saberes*. It awakens in participants a fundamental reverence for who other people are and for what they have to share around the essential mission of bringing forth food for people via an array of agroecological tools, techniques, and relationships.

Research Advocacy—Agroecology advocates for research systems to support the development of clean, sustainable agricultural knowledge and skills. Agroecology establishes production and distribution systems that protect natural resources and reduce greenhouse gas emissions, avoiding energy-intensive industrial methods that damage the environment and the health of those that inhabit it. More and more colleges and universities are establishing degree programs in agroecology.

Basic Nature—Agroecology acknowledges the importance of animals raised for food having the opportunity to live in a way that allows them to express their basic nature rather than being confined in small cages in large industrial factory feeding operations. As agrarian elder Wendell Berry put it, "I dislike the thought that some animal has been made miserable to feed me. If I am going to eat meat, I want it to be from an animal that has lived a pleasant, uncrowded life outdoors, on bountiful pasture, with good water nearby and trees for shade."

Declaration of Nyéléni—A seminal moment in the unfolding story of agroecology came during an international forum held in the village of Nyéléni in Mali, Africa, on February 27, 2007. At that forum, key actors in the global food sovereignty movement came together to write and publish the Nyéléni Declaration.

Here are some key excerpts: "Agroecology means that we stand together in the circle of life, and this implies that we must also stand together in the circle of struggle against land grabbing and the criminalization of our movements.... The vision that animates agroecology is respect for the necessary equilibrium between nature, human beings, and the cosmos. We recognize that as humans we are but a part of nature and the cosmos. We share a spiritual connection with our lands and with the web of life. We reject the commodification of all forms of life."

Nyéléni participants declared that they seek to create a world where "all peoples in each of our countries are able to live with dignity, earn a living wage for their labor, and have the opportunity to remain in their homes.

"Where food sovereignty is a basic human right, recognized and implemented by communities, peoples, states and international bodies.

"Where we are able to conserve and rehabilitate rural environments, fish stocks, landscapes and food tradition based on ecologically sustainable management of land, soils, water, seas, seeds, livestock, and other biodiversity.

"Where peoples' power to make decisions about their material, natural and spiritual heritage are defended."

Structural Changes—The North American Chapter of the Latin American Scientific Society of Agroecology (SOCLA NA) came into being in 2017. It was formed to promote the exchange of agroecological knowledge and wisdom among scientists, farmers, and activists, as well as to help make agroecology a social, political, and academic force.

At the time the North American chapter was launched, founding member Eric Holt-Giménez, executive director of Food First, shared a vision of the social change this new chapter would strive to realize.

Holt-Giménez pointed out that in Latin America, agro-ecology originated as a practice, a science, and a political movement, and that it has challenged the practice and the ideology of industrial agriculture. He wrote that the launch of SOCLA in North America represents the launch of alliances essential to "mobilize social movements, to be a part of social change, and to create the type of political will we need to introduce the tremendous structural changes in land and attitudes."

Cornerstones—In response to hard realities in the realms of economics, environment, climate, and society, agroecology offers a multitude of philosophical and practical paths. Those paths lead away from the constellation of 21st-century crises and toward establishing a clean, sustainable, just agricultural foundation for the whole of culture.

The farm and food movements that are elements of agroecology have a multitude of dimensions: clean land, clean food, human health, animal welfare, worker justice, support for farmers as our ambassadors to the Earth, and more. Agroecological approaches have become so sophisticated and dependable, that they can, as concluded by international studies, supply the clean, healthy food necessary to feed the world. And they can do it while improving soil, air, and water quality, protecting animal and plant species, helping to stabilize Earth's climate, and enhancing human physical and mental health.

As a fundamentally positive and egalitarian movement, agroecological initiatives have the potential to serve nationally and globally as conceptual, philosophical, and practical cornerstones for healthy and spiritually advanced 21st-century civilization.

Crossroads—Agroecology continues to emerge internationally for a host of good reasons, but as the movement has grown, it has been vulnerable to co-optation and corruption, much as the term "natural" has been co-opted. At this point the word natural has been exploited so relentlessly in recent decades that the term is essentially meaningless.

Some agricultural institutions and corporations initially ridiculed or marginalized agroecology. But in recent years they are recognizing that by embracing agroecology as a "marketing concept" and adapting the approach to corporate requirements, they can deflect consumer criticism and thereby stake profitable claims on what they regard as the agroecological "market share." But that is not agroecology at all.

Agroecology, thus, does not mean the same thing everywhere. It is a term that many interests strive to claim for their own purposes. Many governments, international organizations, academics, and corporations have taken up divergent or watered-down approaches to agroecology, but with no shifts in power structures and no true reorientation toward the core ideals of agroecology.

For agroecology to fulfill its potential, we must go way beyond rhetoric and "marketing concepts" to a fundamental realization and appreciation of our relationship with other life forms and the matrix of subtle energies and spiritual realities that characterize our interactions on farm fields, in kitchens, and at dining tables.

The Direction of Knowledge—Olivier De Schutter is cochair of the International Panel of Experts on Sustainable Food Systems (IPES-Food) and a former UN Special Rapporteur on the Right to Food (2008–2014). In a notable review of *Food Sovereignty, Agroecology, and Biocultural Diversity: Constructing and Contesting Knowledge,* he wrote, "We tend to reduce agroecology to a set of agronomic techniques that reduce the need for external inputs, that de-link food production from energy consumption, and that restore soil health. But it is, more fundamentally, about the direction of knowledge: agroecology operates the shift from top-down 'extension' of knowledge by experts delegated by ministries, to a bottom-up approach prioritizing the local knowledge developed by farmers. It is empowering, horizontal, based on trial and error—but it is also another way of conceiving science."

At this juncture, the leading edge of agroecology practice in North America comprises organic, regenerative, and biodynamic farms, food co-ops, CSAs, farmers markets, urban ag initiatives, farmworker movements, local food policy councils, food hubs, open-source food networks, and so forth. They are complemented by developing university programs. As our global situation intensifies, the movement toward agroecology requires many more individuals, communities, and institutions to take up the cause and the practice.

Agroecology engages technical, social, cultural, scientific, and political possibilities and practicalities. Deep agroecology embraces all this, and gives open, discerning attention to the subtle dimensions that underlie every outward expression.

Chapter 4

Webs of Light and Life

*"The light of our land becomes the light of our food
becomes the light of our lives."*

—Paolo Manzelli

In daily life our focus tends to be on the visible. But the invisible is also real, as we know from the simple experience of feeling warmth radiate from a fire. More subtly, have you ever had the experience of sitting somewhere in public and then, feeling something, turned your head to find that someone was staring at you? Or have you been caught in the act of gawking? How did they know? How did you know?

Invisible forces—dimensions of light in particular—play a key role in our lives on a fundamental level through our farms and our food. All the universe is alive, intelligent, permeated with life force. We live our lives in a matrix of interweaving energies, some generated from nature and some from technology. Explorations of the subatomic world have in recent decades revolutionized our comprehension of how the universe exists and how it unfolds.

These basic observations are essential to acknowledge before considering how deep agroecology may extend the healing initiatives of agroecology. It's a foundational reality: the relationship of light with our earthly substance and sustenance. Deep agroecology depends upon recognition of, and respect for, our personal energetic realities and their manifold webs of entanglement with land, farms, farmers, cooks, food, and the cosmos. When we are respectfully aware of and cooperating intelligently with both gross and subtle life forces to provide food, fiber, and beauty, we are practicing deep agroecology.

In striving with this book to encourage bridges of understanding and right relationship among particle and wave, science and intuition, material and mystery, I am relying ultimately on the deep and beautiful native teachings that I've been privileged to engage in over the course of my life. That part of the deep agroecology story comes later, after some essential explorations into the physics of the subtle realms.

This chapter is a nonlinear exploration of realities and possibilities, not a grand theory of subtle energy and agriculture. Any such theory would likely soon be outdated. The pace of discovery and learning in these matters is swift, and the subject is not now amenable to being defined in static terms.

The Unseen Exists—For deep agroecology to be understood and applied, there must be evolutionary steps forward and upward in our individual and collective lives. Among the important steps, human beings must overcome the limiting fiction that material measure is all there is. There is a relationship between human states of consciousness and the material world. As author Richard Ford expressed it in *The Lay of the Land*, "The unseen exists and it has properties."

We human beings require nourishment not just for our bodies but also for our psyches. This can come most healthfully through relationships with nature—a tangible experience of one's own life force being nourished by the unseen life force of plants, animals, and the planet itself. It's something that we all intuit.

Panpsychism—According to the *Stanford Encyclopedia of Philosophy*, "panpsychism" refers to the viewpoint that everything we encounter—from a cloud to a tree to a pebble—has a mind. Intelligence of various kinds and qualities is fundamental and ubiquitous in the natural world.

The panpsychic viewpoint has a venerable history in philosophical traditions of both East and West, as well as the North and South. That recognition in the West dates back at least as far as 644 BCE among the group of Greek philosophers who preceded Socrates. The recognition came earlier in the East, and earlier than that in native lands of all directions, 12,000 years or more among the native philosophers of Turtle Island (North America).

As with the Gaia hypothesis, panpsychism offers a unified conception of nature. Its integrative proposition is that consciousness is a fundamental feature of physical matter. Every single particle in existence has at minimum a simple spark of consciousness. Those particles can and do enter into relationships to establish more complex forms of consciousness.

Metanoia—In the time of classical Greek civilization (fifth and fourth centuries BCE), awakening to new perceptions of reality was referred to as *metanoia*. The word also connoted the natural phenomenon of spiritual awakening, the capacity to see things in a new, enhanced light.

As I've observed over the decades of my own life, and as I have at times experienced, in counterpoint to soul states of awakening and clarity, there can occur states of dullness. They arise from oversaturation or persistent toxicity. And saturation and toxicity can often be traced to long-term dysfunctional dietary patterns. In addition to the dulling, as I've observed directly, steady ingestion of bad food can also impart hardening to the soul, making it difficult for light to penetrate and for metanoia to evolve.

Quantum Theory—Sometimes spoken of as "quantum mechanics" or "matrix mechanics," the realm of quantum theory has been developing exponentially over the last century, dating back to the work of Max Planck and Albert Einstein. Quantum is a generally accepted theory in physics, a branch of study relating to the infinitesimally small. It's a theory of how atoms, molecules, and other physical manifestations at that invisible (to us) scale actually operate. Turns out they do not obey Newtonian mechanics, such as the familiar example of an apple falling to the ground rather than to the sky. Quantum reality is different. At the quantum scale, everything exists and operates in respect to something known as the uncertainty principle.

Uncertainty—The uncertainty principle came forward in the field of physics almost a hundred years ago in recognition that quantum theory has limits in relation to the precision with which quantities can be known. There is always a degree of uncertainty. Objects express duality, which is to say they have the characteristics of both waves and particles. Are they one, or the other, or both? All matter and energy behave sometimes like particles, bit by bit, and sometimes like waves, smooth and continuous.

Quantum mechanics challenges our common-sense grasp of what things are and what they can do. The scientist who developed the uncertainty principle in 1927,

Werner Heisenberg, said that quantum particles are not definably real but rather that "they form a world of potentialities or possibilities, rather than one of things or facts." Our interaction, even just as observers, changes the nature of reality. Author and *New York Times* book reviewer James Gleick called this "a no-man's-land between philosophy and religion."

Our evolving grasp of quantum theory has so far led to important applications in quantum chemistry, quantum optics, quantum computing, superconducting magnets, light-emitting diodes, lasers, transistors, semiconductors, magnetic resonance imaging (MRI), and electron microscopy.

Entanglement—*Entanglement* is the word applied to one of the main principles of quantum physics. It seeks to describe a physical phenomenon that occurs when pairs or groups of particles interact. The quantum state of each particle cannot be described independently of the others. The quantum state of one particle determines the possible quantum states of the other particles. Relationship is integral.

In the realm of quantum mechanics, the observations of entanglement inform us that certain particles behave as a single unified system even when they're separated by immense distances. The theory holds that two entangled photons react without any delay if one of the photons is affected. It matters not where the other photon is in the universe, even if located millions of miles away. This quantum reality—that there can be communication and relationship between particles separated by vast distances—has naturally inspired many theorists to suggest that the universe exists as, and functions as, a fundamental whole rather than as a collection of discrete parts.

Photons—The same year that Albert Einstein proposed the theory of special relativity, 1905, he also defined a new discovery: a unit of light he called a "light quantum." Today we speak of this natural phenomenon as *photons*.

A photon is a bit of light energy that has no mass yet acts like a particle and that moves at the speed of light (186,282 miles per second). Energy exchange between any object in the universe and any other object is done by sharing photons.

Biophotons—The sparks of light and life generated from within biological systems are called biophotons. They are used by and stored in all organisms, including the food we eat, the water we drink, the air we breathe, and our bodies. At the same time, all living cells emit biophotons, which cannot be seen by the naked eye but which can be measured by special equipment. It's an invisible and ongoing biophotonic dance between us and the rest of the world. When our food is vibrant with high-quality life energy (biophotons), that energy (not just the material substance of vitamins and minerals) is absorbed. It makes a subtle but important difference.

Beings of Light—Physicist Fritz-Albert Popp, PhD, of Germany's Marburg University, researched living light. He is the person who named the natural phenomenon *biophotons*, and his pioneering work has been accepted by a wide segment of the scientific community. Popp found that biophotons were coherent, and he suggested that they may in fact regulate the life processes of an organism. He famously observed, "We know today that man essentially, is a being of light."

Chi—The importance of biophotonic life force, usually spoken of as basic life force, has been known for centuries around the world. In China it is called *chi*, in Japan *ki*. The Sanskrit term is *prana*, and it's *kupuri* among the Huichol people of the Sierra Madre mountains in the western states of Mexico. Other native peoples of the Americas as well as the wider world know it by other names. In recent decades, especially since the wide acceptance of acupuncture with its sophisticated understanding of human energy systems, Western science has increasingly recognized the reality of the animating life force.

Light and Life—Fritz-Albert Popp was among the first Western investigators to theorize that this light must come, at least in part, from the foods we eat. The more light a food is able to store, the more nutritious it is. Naturally grown fresh fruits and vegetables, for example, are rich in biophotons. You need not be an adept who can see auras to perceive this. The reality of light waves, or biophoton energy, is plain to a relaxed, receptive, and discerning eye.

Biophotons elevate an organism—such as your physical body—to a higher oscillation. If you eat fresh, clean food grown on healthy, natural land, you are supporting your body at a higher, healthier vibe. The greater your supply of living light force from fresh, clean foods, water, and air, the greater the potential vitality of your overall electromagnetic field (aura) and, consequently, the more energy available for maintaining optimal health. In matters biophotonic, quality as much as quantity is key.

"We are still on the threshold of fully understanding the complex relationship between light and life," Popp observed, "but we can now say emphatically, that the function of our entire metabolism is dependent on light."

Cellular Communication—In a 2012 article about biophoton communication published in *MIT Technology Review*, the authors cited a growing body of evidence suggesting that the molecular machinery of life both absorbs and emits photons. One biologist found evidence that this light is a new form of cellular communication, analogous to the 1s and 0s of binary code that communicate through the whole vast reach of the World Wide Web.

Coherent—In "Speculations about Bystander and Biophotons," a paper published in the National Institutes of Health journal *Dose-Response*, author Charles L. Sanders writes: "...the last hundred years have shown that cells and now whole animals may communicate with each other by electromagnetic waves called biophotons...These ultra-weak photons are coherent, appear to originate and concentrate in DNA of the cell nucleus, and rapidly carry large amounts of data to each cell and to the trillions of other cells in the human body."

He speculated that perhaps our human spirit and consciousness communicates with our bodies through biophotons. "Maybe there is a world that exists within light," Sanders writes, "and no matter where you are in The Universe photons can act as portals that enable communication between these two worlds?"

How Now—When I sat with friend Doug Dittman one afternoon in the kitchen at his Branched Oak Farm in Raymond, Nebraska, he told me that he takes a long view. He reminded me that glaciers have scraped and shaped the Nebraska landscape four times in the geologic past, and they may come again. Also, three times in the past, vast saline oceans sat right here, by precise geolocation, where he and I were sitting at his kitchen table.

"I have that history in mind," Doug told me. "I know that. I look at the long stretch of it, and I want to do what I can to be helpful. Everyone has a different path, a different ability. When I look at these paddocks out here, for me the three big issues are bur oaks, quartzite boulders, and jersey cows, jersey brown cows. They are a very thrifty animal. They can get you to wondering, why are all the ruminants on the Great Plains brown? Well, I suppose, nature chose that color outside of cognition because it has something to do with light absorption and reflection. It has to do with the light."

Brain Light—Scientists have discovered biophotons in the brain that suggest our consciousness is directly linked to light. They have found, for example, that neurons in mammalian brains are capable of producing biophotons. Notably, the photons appear within the visible spectrum. Some researchers have an informed suspicion that our brain's neurons are capable of communicating through light. They hypothesize that the brain might have optical communication channels.

In a number of experiments, scientists found that rat brains can pass just one biophoton per neuron a minute, whereas human brains can convey more than a billion biophotons per second. This raises a question. Could it be possible that the more light a human being can produce and thereby communicate between neurons, the more awake or conscious they are? Does such an awake state convey an evolutionary survival advantage, or disadvantage?

Light Has Its Own Life—"Here is a concept from Iroquois cosmology which might explain many physical phenomena: Light has awareness, light has consciousness. Light is its own life."—Doug George-Kanentiio, Mohawk

Natural Mystic—Meditation masters in the world's spiritual traditions have spoken throughout history of an inner light that pervades the physical and energy bodies. Mystics have often equated this pervasive light with primordial consciousness and the source of life as well as matter. Whether we look outside into our environment or inside into ourselves, we find primordial light.

Halo—Over the centuries, the world has accumulated a wealth of paintings, and firsthand reports, of the halo phenomenon. These images and reports establish that throughout history in a wide range of cultures scattered around the world, people have perceived a shining crown of light, a halo, around the heads of particularly kind, wise, compassionate, and sanctified individuals.

The familiar halo could also be described as a radiant nimbus of biophotons. Many would say this is light generated from steady, consistent, generous, loving thought, others adding the notion that halos are the visible product of a certain level of consciousness above thought.

Triune Brain—The American physician and neuroscientist Paul D. McLean (1913–2007) posited that within our skulls, we human beings harbor what he dubbed "the triune brain." McLean theorized that the human brain was composed of three components that had evolved over different periods and now worked together as one: the reptilian complex, the limbic system, and the neocortex. Some neuroscientists regard McLean's model as oversimplified. However, while technically inaccurate in some respects, it continues to offer a useful explanatory framework.

In McLean's conception, the *reptilian brain* refers to those brain structures related to territoriality, ritual behavior, and other reptile-like instincts and behaviors. The *limbic brain* refers to those brain structures, wherever located, associated with social and nurturing behaviors, mutual reciprocity, and other habits and affects that evolved during the age of the mammals. And the *neocortex* represents that cluster of brain structures involved in advanced cognition, including planning, modeling, and simulation.

Floral Brain—In *Jitterbug Perfume*, novelist Tom Robbins speculates that the third brain, the neocortex, can be thought of as a "floral" brain. Physically, the neocortex is a dense rind of nerve fibers about an inch thick. It's molded over the top of the mammal brain (midbrain or mesencephalon). In many ways, it parallels the way flowers function.

As flowers extract energy and information from light, likewise neuromelanin (one of the principal chemicals in the neocortex) absorbs light and also has the capacity to convert light into other forms of energy. The neocortex is literally light sensitive and can be lit up by higher forms of mental activity such as meditation, chanting, or profound beauty in nature or art. Thus, Robbins writes, "[T]he ancients were not being metaphorical when they referred to 'illumination.'"

The novelist speculates that as we continue to evolve and our neocortex comes into full use, we too will practice a kind of photosynthesis like the flowers. "With reptile consciousness," Robbins concludes, "we had hostile confrontation. With mammal consciousness, we had civilized debate. With floral consciousness, we'll have empathic telepathy."

The Fifth Element—When I interviewed Carlos Barrios back in 2002, he told me that he was born into a Spanish family on El Altiplano, the highlands of Guatemala.

His home was in Huehuetenango, also the dwelling place of the Maya Mam peoples. With other Maya and other indigenous tradition keepers, the Mam carry knowledge of an important part of the old ways of the high civilizations presiding on Turtle Island (North America) before the invasions of colonial armies and settlers. Barrios told me that he is a historian, an anthropologist, and a student of the mysteries. After studying with traditional elders for 25 years, since the age of 19, Barrios says he also became a Mayan *Ajq'ij*, a ceremonial priest and spiritual guide, Eagle Clan.

Barrios told me that according to his understanding of the Mayan calendar, the emerging era of time is calling attention to a much-overlooked element. Whereas the four traditional elements of earth, air, fire, and water have dominated various epochs in the past, there will be a fifth dimension, a fifth element to reckon with in the time of the Fifth Sun: ether. The dictionary defines ether as the rarefied element thought to fill the upper regions of space, the heavens. Ether is a medium that permeates all space and transmits waves of energy in a wide range of frequencies. What is "ethereal" is related to the regions beyond Earth: the heavens.

Ether—According to Mesoamerican cosmology, ether/akasha is the fifth element of the Fifth Sun, which is recognized in their elaborate calendric systems as the era of time now commencing.

Celestial, and lacking in material substance, ether is thought to be no less real than wood, wind, flame, stone, or flesh. Aristotle held that the heavens are made of a special weightless and incorruptible fifth element called "aether." The word *aether* in Homeric Greek means "pure, fresh air" or "clear sky."

In Greek mythology, ether was thought to be the pure essence that the gods breathed, filling the Olympian heights they inhabited. In Roman times, ether also bore the name "quintessence," meaning, literally, "fifth being."

Fields—We arise from and are sustained by field phenomena, waveforms of biophotonic light and sound, which form our essential nature through acoustic holography. Biologist Dr. Bruce Lipton speaks of this as an equation (matter + field = structure).

Just as the invisible force field of a magnet will cause bits of iron filings to assume a distinct pattern in accord with the force field, a multitude of other invisible fields of energy give shape to the material world. Albert Einstein himself acknowledged this reality when he wrote: "The field is the sole governing agency of the particle."

Global Resonance—As scientists have long observed, the Earth itself has its own particular energy vibration and field. This is sometimes called the Worldwide Hum or the Schumann resonances (SR). They are numbers representing a set of spectrum peaks in the extremely low frequency (ELF) portion of the Earth's electromagnetic field. Earth's aura is the geomagnetic field that extends from our planet's core out into space.

An invisible electromagnetic cocoon surrounding the Earth, the Van Allen belt, was discovered in 1958 by scientific instruments carried aboard NASA's first successful satellite launch, Explorer 1. The Van Allen radiation belt is a zone of energetically charged particles, most of which originate from the solar wind that is captured by and held around Earth by our planet's magnetic field. In space, our planetary aura meets and interacts with the solar wind, a stream of charged particles emanating from the Sun.

Entangled with all of this is yet more energy that we must classify as subtle: a vast, relentless influx of electromagnetics from our local galactic field, and no doubt from precincts and galaxies far beyond our familiar Milky Way neighborhood. Whether you elect to call this enveloping web of light and energy "intelligent quantum-active energy dynamics," or spirit forces, it is a fact of our lives. Cooperating intelligently with it constitutes a giant and necessary step forward in human evolution. That's part of deep agroecology.

A Great Thought—"The stream of knowledge is heading towards a non-mechanical reality; the universe begins to look more like a great thought than a great machine," observed Sir James Jeans.

Power of Intention—Author Lynne McTaggart and psychologist Gary Schwartz began conducting a series of Germination Intention Experiments (GIE) at the University of Arizona in 2007. They set out to test whether human intention could affect the growth of plants and, if so, to further explore the concept that *thought is a thing* and that it impacts other things.

They ran six experiments: one via the internet with participants from all over the world and five others in front of live audiences. Based on their experiments and their understanding of additional research conducted at Princeton, MIT, Stanford, and other universities and laboratories, they concluded that the universe is connected—everything to everything—through a vast quantum energy field.

The GIEs set up by McTaggart and Schwartz were large-scale, mind-over-matter experiments that they say provided evidence that intention can affect distant targets. The first tests examined whether intention could alter the tiny light (biophoton emissions) emitted from living things. They chose a simple geranium leaf as a focal point for the attendees of a conference held in London. The 400 attendees were asked to send the intention to increase the light emissions of a geranium leaf at the University of Arizona—to make the leaf "glow and glow." Meanwhile, in the laboratory in Arizona, they used highly sensitive CCD cameras, ordinarily used to record and photograph the faint light of outer space, to record even the most infinitesimal changes.

The result of the group's focused intention was strong enough to be readily observable in the digital images. The increased biophoton effect had high statistical significance compared to the control. After running six experiments with significant results, McTaggart and Schwartz concluded that the focused intention from a group can affect living light in everything from algae and leaves to human beings.

Guiding Force—Each cell in the body emits more than 100,000 light impulses per second. These biophotonic light emissions arise from all living things, not just human beings. They have been found to be a guiding force behind all of the body's biochemical reactions. The emission of light particles (biophotons) may well be the mechanism, so to speak, through which an intention produces its effects.

Quantum Agriculture—On his website and in his book *Quantum Agriculture*, farmer and farming consultant Hugh Lovel describes a new, evolving method of agriculture. He applies the last century of discoveries in quantum physics and quantum biology to growing food.

"*Quantum Agriculture* not only considers the chemistry and life of soil biology," he writes, "but also the warmth and light of the atmosphere and how this interacts with nitrogen, oxygen, moisture, and carbon dioxide to provide 95 percent or more of the make-up of plants and animals." Quantum agriculture strives toward self-sufficiency, abundance, and restoration of soil fertility to aid in sequestering carbon and reversing global warming.

As Lovel explains it, quantum agriculture looks at the role of energy and asks what are the dynamics? What processes are going on? "If the right processes are happening in your paddock," he writes, "then the biology will follow along with the processes. And if the biology follows along, then the minerals will follow along, too. So you want to have some way of working with the energetics of your farm, because then you can do more for less."

In-form-ation—Biodynamic agriculture is one agroecological system for working more consciously with subtle forces. In the autumn of 2016 during an outdoor seminar at Santa Fe Community College, Hugh Lovel said the biodynamic method "grows food and medicine for human evolution."

He explained that the herbal and mineral preparations used by biodynamic farmers and gardeners, preparations sprayed upon the land in quantum amounts, are essentially organizing principles. "You can't see them," he said, "but they are at work." He offered the analogy of the music played at a dance. At first, everyone at the dance is just standing around awkwardly. But then the band starts playing, and the music acts as an organizing principle. Everyone starts moving, dancing to the music. You can't see it, but still it is organizing, and people are responding.

Likewise, he explained, the substances in biodynamic preparations embody archetypal patterns—organizing principles. When biodynamic preparations are added to a bucket of water, and then stirred rhythmically for an extended period of time, the interchanging vortices created by the stirring organize the water in a particular way. When finished, the energized preparation is loaded into a sprayer and the droplets then go out over fields and gardens, establishing a web of microscopic hubs bearing intention and information. The micro-droplets attract and organize energy based around their inherent and now-activated archetypal patterns.

"Spirit has information," Lovel said. "The substance of the preparations provides form for the spirit when they are brought together in a vortex. In this manner the farmers or gardeners establish *in-form-ation* that is beneficial to the healthy development of soils and plants."

Obscurations—It's a near metaphysical certainty that obscurations will arise. There are a great number of factors, personal and global, that can darken our capacity to perceive clearly what is going on. For example, we live in the modern milieu of electromagnetic waves. Cell phone, radio, Wi-Fi, TV, and more. We are immersed in invisible, entangled waves and fields of techno-generated energy that does influence us in ways lesser and greater. In context of this, we are challenged to see, to know, and to understand accurately, and to make wise decisions.

"Something as mundane as a microwave oven or smart refrigerator can send out radio signals that blind sophisticated interstellar radio telescopes and so make it impossible to receive the energy coming down from the stars," author David Spangler has observed. "Such instruments can likewise blind human beings to receiving the light coming down from the stars."

It's easy for us human beings to be distracted from the subtle and supersensible worlds and for our human faculties to become dulled or hardened. Obscurations that can arise from poor diet or the techno-matrix can be cleared, but that clearing requires intention and discipline. Traditional wisdom keepers from around the world have perennially advised that spending time in nature is a key antidote in this regard, a sensible and accessible way to dispel obscurations and to grasp what is real and truly important.

Prelude to Deep Agroecology—This chapter's nonlinear exploration of subtle energies has been a necessary prelude to consideration of deep agroecology. We human beings have the capacity to influence the world not just with our physical actions and sophisticated tools but also with the light of our creative thoughts, feelings, intentions, and words. This holds true across the realms of engagement, stretching from farm fields and feedlots to kitchen counters, on to our household dining tables.

Deep agroecology recognizes, acknowledges, and strives to cooperate intelligently with these forces and forms. Subtle realms are terra incognita for most of the modern world at the moment, but they are the fields in which deep agroecology has its place and in which it strives to have an intelligent and productive impact. I believe that as people enter these fields, they will find that they are altogether natural, welcoming, and fertile.

Chapter 5

Elements of Deep Agroecology

"Genius ... arises in the natural, aboriginal concern for the conscious unity of all phenomena."

—Mary Hunter Austin

Environmental and economic realities are pushing us hard to enact a more intelligent way of drawing our life from the land. That intelligence cannot be limited to material, mechanical, mathematical, efficiency-dominated systems. Such a limited approach would be tragically inadequate. Along with ethical science and technology, we need also a feeling, intuitive, nurturing, wholehearted, respectful, and intelligent visionary engagement with land, life, and the cosmic matrix of subtle energies that weave it whole. That would be an expression of spiritual maturity on a cultural level, and it absolutely requires a radiantly healthy agricultural foundation.

To reach toward these necessary ideals, our approach must also be characterized by agroecological precepts such as free will, food democracy, and full respect and economic justice for all, including our relatives who tend the earth on our behalf and who prepare the food for our tables. These are primary values. A decisive part of the pathway toward these ideals can come from agroecology and deep agroecology.

Deep agroecology is a response to the climate, chemical, and cultural crises unfolding in the world. In my conception, deep agroecology ratifies and embraces the ideas and approaches of agroecology and strives to call wide public attention to the healing agrarian pathways it represents. Further, deep agroecology explores realms of subtle energy and their consequential influence on farms, food, and people, showing how native wisdom ways can help guide both cultural and agricultural practices along necessary evolutionary pathways.

In writing about deep agroecology I hope to help inspire a vast network of agrarian-environmental oases, where farms and farm life have cultivated a radiance that uplifts everything in a way similar to the way great works of art or masterpieces of music lift the people who come in contact with them. This is possible. This is necessary. This is worth reaching for.

In describing the deep agroecology ideal, I'm mindful of the counsel offered to me one afternoon by my friend, dairyman Doug Dittman of Branched Oak Farm in Raymond, Nebraska.

"One of the intrinsic problems of farming," Doug told me, "is that you are constantly in the trenches. There are so many demands in the field, or in the barn. I mean, the cows have to be milked. You can't not milk them. When you are in farming there's little wiggle room. In the trenches you can grasp idyllic conceptions of farming, and they may have strong appeal. You can see the directions you need to go ecologically. But it's really hard to get to it when you have so many demands, and a mortgage that you need to pay."

Of course, Doug is right. The ideal is really hard to get to, always just out of reach. But as is evident when surveying Branched Oak Farm, Doug has made giant strides toward the ideal by having and holding a vision he has followed though his career. Part of his vision over 25 years or more has been to create a forest of bur oak, trees that can live for up to 500 years (about 20 generations). Every year he has faithfully planted saplings of bur oak (*quercus macrocarpa*). The trees have slowly, steadily grown toward expression of their archetype of massive trunk and wide, open crown.

Doug's vision guided him to establish and maintain a beautiful, clean, productive, and organically certified dairy farm, creamery, and forest, all while remaining actively engaged in the local community. Similarly, I hope the vision of deep agroecology can inspire and help guide many others forward in the overall farm and food movement. If you want to realize a vision, you've got to have a vision first. Deep agroecology is an effort to encourage and enlarge the public conversation about elements of agroecology in the hope that the vision can be grasped and pursued more widely in the Americas and around the world.

To help clarify for the public the importance and the vision of agroecology, I offer in this chapter an expansion of the subject into deeper, less discussed, and perhaps more mysterious dimensions of the relationship matrix that extends from the soil to the supper table. The elements and practices of agroecology and deep agroecology can well serve our next natural, and necessary, evolutionary step as a community of living beings on a finite planet. For the sake of clarifying the vision, I propose the following elements of deep agroecology.

ELEMENTS

Agriculture—Agriculture is the foundation supporting civilization. In our era it's a vast global matrix of arts and sciences for cultivating land, raising crops, and controlling animals for food. The first agriculture appears to have developed toward the end of the Last Glacial Period, about 11,700 years ago. Temperatures warmed, glaciers melted, sea levels rose, and ecosystems everywhere on Earth adapted and reorganized. Human beings also adapted their survival practices of hunting and gathering and set down roots. As people began to cultivate the earth, they also cultivated culture itself, leading onward to our present circumstances.

Ecology—Ecology is the scientific study of the relationships among living organisms and their environment, an interdisciplinary field of signal importance. Some scholars suggest that ecology had its philosophical and practical origins in classical Greek culture, the era of Aristotle (384–322 BCE) and Theophrastus of Eresos. A student of Aristotle, Theophrastus produced many important works, including a systematic study of 500 plants. He's often cited as the father of both botany and ecology.

In our times, ecology is a highly developed field of science that includes biology, botany, geography, Earth science, and more. In some contexts, it's also a political movement that seeks to protect the environment from pollution, overexploitation, and general degradation.

According to the *Encyclopaedia Britannica*, "some of the most pressing problems in human affairs—expanding populations, food scarcities, environmental pollution, including global warming, extinctions of plant and animal species, and all the attendant sociological and political problems—are to a great degree ecological."

Deep Ecology—In the 1970s the ideas of deep ecology evolved out of the core concepts of ecology. As a philosophy, it extended ecology by acknowledging the inherent worth of all life forms regardless of their utility for human needs or desires. Deep ecology pointed out that the natural world is a subtle balance of complex interrelationships in which organisms depend on each other for their existence within ecosystems. Relationship is an essential factor in ecological well-being.

Norwegian philosopher Arne Naess (1912–2009), a widely respected figure within the environmental movement, coined the phrase "deep ecology" and gave passionate and scholarly expression to the idea. He recognized that human destruction of the natural world was posing a grave threat not just to human beings but also to other living creatures. Essential ecological relationships were being extinguished on an industrial scale.

He wrote, "Present human interference with the non-human world is excessive, and the situation is rapidly worsening." Professor Naess argued that the environmental and ecological approaches had so far been shallow, addressing symptoms but not root causes. Naess recognized the necessity of going deeper. He argued that resolving the environmental crisis was not just a question of technology but rather required a fundamental shift in the way we see and engage with the world. From that realization (*metanoia*) could come essential changes in policy and practice for economic and technological systems.

Roots—In employing the word "deep" to describe the direction he felt ecology needed to pursue, Naess raised elemental questions about our purposes and values when we plan, develop, or engage in any action that impacts the web of natural relationships. Naess advocated going to the core of problems and reckoning directly with the roots rather than forever mopping up the micro- and macro-messes of modern civilization.

Importantly, Naess opposed the notion that resolving the environmental crisis was simply a matter of creating better technology. He considered this to be a shallow approach because such "fixes" tended to stop before fundamental change. He meant technological fixes such as recycling, cleaning up toxic spills, improving gas mileage in autos, or shifting to forms of agriculture that may not employ toxic chemicals but do use a monocultural approach dependent on exports.

In distinction, deep ecology as he conceived of it involves redesigning whole systems based on values and methods that truly preserve the ecological and cultural diversity of natural systems.

With American philosopher and environmentalist George Sessions, Naess developed an eight-tier platform to explain deep ecology. The platform included the idea that the well-being and flourishing of human and non-human life on Earth have value in themselves. "These values are independent of the usefulness of the non-human world for human purposes... Richness and diversity of life forms contribute to the realization of these values and are also values in themselves."

Enlightened Self-Interest—"A great challenge of today," Naess wrote, "is to save the planet from further devastation that violates both the enlightened self-interest of humans and non-humans, and decreases the potential of joyful existence for all." He wrote those words decades ago. Over time reality has revealed them as even more starkly true.

By developing our capacity to see, grasp, and identify with reality, particularly the reality of the natural world we inhabit, we are motivated to intelligent action. That approach, in the words of Naess, is "deepened realism."

Naess felt that appeals for people to exhibit moral-intelligent behavior were impotent in the face of the steady, helter-skelter derangement of the planet and that such appeals tended to have little impact. Instead, he saw that human beings are more likely to change through encouragement, and through going deeper to truly know ourselves (self-realization). In defending the Earth, we are defending ourselves.

Deep realism, self-realization, mutual encouragement, and deep ecology are all elements of deep agroecology.

Value in All Life—Dolores LaChapelle, author of *Sacred Land, Sacred Sex* and other works concerning deep ecology, wrote that a basic point of deep ecology is to recognize and to respect the reality that there is intrinsic value in all life. "Diversity, symbiosis, and thus complexity characterize the life of nature itself. Humanity is part of nature...."

Spiritual Intelligence—Biodynamic farmer Hugh Lovel expressed an interesting view while leading a workshop in Santa Fe back in 2016. He said, "Observation is the basis of intelligence, while understanding is the basis of integrity. Where the attention goes the energy flows. Accurate intervention to augment natural processes requires keen observation, along with an understanding of nature, so that exact diagnosis and appropriate responses occur."

In Lovel's view, combining observation with meditation helps inform appropriate activity on the land, farm, garden, orchard, or forest. "The brain and the heart are both intelligent organs," he said. "It's worthwhile to spend time developing both."

Triple Bottom Line—The business term *bottom line* refers specifically to the profit and loss statement. What is the final monetary outcome of the enterprise? In most cases, the bottom line is the major factor for a wide range of business decisions. By contrast, food co-ops and many other responsible businesses have for five decades embraced a basic sustainability concept that's now known as the *triple bottom line* (TBL). That's an accounting framework with three considerations: financial, environmental, and social, sometimes referenced as economy, equity, and ecology.

Businesses adopt the TBL framework to give them a context for evaluating their operations, upholding values such as fairness and environmental responsibility, and also to enhance the value of their businesses. This is full-cost accounting. For example, if a corporation shows a bottom-line monetary profit but their industry fouls a river with chemical toxins, and the taxpayers wind up suffering the health consequences and also paying the bill for river cleanup, that's profitable for the business but ruinous for the community. In such an instance, the bottom line alone is an inadequate and unjust way of evaluating the company's performance.

Quadruple Bottom Line—To augment the accounting parameters of TBL, some enterprises have added a fourth bottom line. Not just economy, equity, and ecology but also creative expression. Angelic Organics in Caledonia, Illinois, for example, works to lift up the understanding that agriculture includes culture and an enlivening range of creative human expression. Regenerative agriculture, the thinking goes, must include celebration of creative expression. It can't be just work.

Angelic Organics Farm and Learning Center has been a leader in this regard, striving in recent years toward a *quadruple bottom line*. Executive director Thomas Spaulding says that local sustainable food and farm systems should strive to meet not just the triple bottom line but also extend their vision and activities into the realm of creative human expression.

"In a materialistic culture," Spaulding has written, "lifting up human expression and culture, freedom of expression, is very important. If our farms are deadened factories that meet guidelines for taking care of the Earth, have great profit and loss statements, take care of animals well, and pay just wages, then we can still end up cold and deadened as people and as communities. We need to lift up and defend the highest of human aspirations—to be fully expressed as spiritual beings."

Love Is the Altar—My wife, Elizabeth, and I drove from Lincoln, Nebraska, to Kansas City, Missouri, in April of 2014. We had tickets to hear Dr. Vandana Shiva give a talk on farms and food. When she took the stage to begin her presentation at Kansas City Unity Temple, she swept her arm back, gesturing to a stained-glass window depicting a star burst with the word *love* spelled out. "That's it," she said. "Love. Love is the altar. It's all about love, about bestowing attention, fostering, cherishing, honoring, tending, guarding, and loving the Earth, which provides our food. The only way we can cultivate that essential ingredient of love is with community and diversity."

"For a short time," Shiva continued, "the mechanistic mind has projected onto the world the false idea that food production is and must be of necessity an industrial activity. That's a world view that is in profound error.... When food becomes a commodity it loses its quality, its taste, and its capacity to provide true nutrition. Industrial agriculture turns the Earth into units of production, farmers into high-tech sharecroppers, and is the single biggest contributor to our declining environment. Industrial agriculture distorts the proper relationship between humans and the natural world."

Simplicity—A physicist by training, Dr. Shiva became an activist for small-scale, decentralized sustainable agriculture in 1987. One-dimensional, profit-based thinking is the core of what Shiva wrote about in her seminal 1993 book, *Monocultures of the Mind.* Coming at the subject from her understanding of particle physics, quantum mechanics, and the fundamental inseparability of all facets of life, she concluded that "issues about environment, economics, and politics are interrelated through the way humans interact with their surroundings and with each other."

"A monoculture of the mind in the economic system is what has led to corporate globalization," she said in her Kansas City talk. "A monoculture of the mind makes it appear as if the only market that there is, is the globalized market controlled by the global giants, whereas the real market, and the real economy, are the economies of nature. That is where local food movements and systems are becoming the solution to the multiple crises created by the monoculture monopoly system."

"We need to shift the paradigm of economics to measure the well-being of people," she said, "not the profits of the oligarchs." This might well be called a *polyculture of the mind.*

"Simplicity is the highest order—the simplicity of good food, safe food, and food produced and consumed in love," Shiva said. "This can only come out of community. Cultivate compassion, love, and food democracy. Food democracy is about action, changing the way we eat every time we take a bite. It's about people learning, engaging, and acting in our food systems."

Feminine Spirit—The worldwide exploitation and despoliation of the Earth and its resources is paralleled in the global exploitation of women, including psychological, physical, economic, and social violence. These are gross injustices that perpetuate and exacerbate gross imbalances in planet and culture.

Global food security depends on the wholesome empowerment of women as human beings and respect for the life they make possible. As farmers, workers, and entrepreneurs, women make essential contributions in agriculture and rural enterprise. Their roles vary across regions but, everywhere, women face legal, economic, and social constraints that harm them and the well-being of their families, communities, and nations and hamper their empowerment.

As detailed in a 2019 FAO report, *The State of Food and Agriculture: Women in Agriculture*, compared to men, women and girls are more severely affected by poverty, hunger, and disease. When food is scarce, female family members often get the smallest portions. In Africa and much of Asia, women constitute the majority of the agricultural labor force in rural areas and also bear main responsibility for taking care of children and elderly.

While women make essential contributions to agriculture, they often lack access to land, education, financial services, farm animals, technology, and other critical resources. These injustices against women hold the world back. According to the FAO, closing the gender gap in agriculture could lift many millions of people out of hunger and also provide positive secondary effects, such as healthier children and families.

As various elders have said to me over the decades, the feminine spirit is rising in our era toward respect, balance, inclusion. This is a healthy and inevitable force now alive in the world, and the rising continues despite a vast array of forces seeking to overwhelm or thwart it. Life depends upon this, and this feminine spirit is an essential, multi-faceted element of deep agroecology.

Cosmic Nutrition—With a series of lectures in 1924, Austrian scientist and philosopher Rudolf Steiner (1861 –1925) planted a seed. His lectures were collected in *The Agriculture Course*. From that beginning, the seeds have grown into the worldwide biodynamic farming and gardening movement, one dynamic model of the many creative initiatives toward deep agroecology that are now arising globally.

Among the many pictures Steiner offered up in his lectures was an agrarian image of artfully supporting plants to be more intelligent in receiving what he called "cosmic nutrition"—subtle forces from the realms beyond Earth, what some refer to as "condensed light." As explored in the previous chapter, that cosmic light has an impact on all the natural world, including human beings.

Ludwig Andreas Feuerbach, a German philosopher, is often credited with being one of the originators of the idea that "you are what you eat." This basic observation, echoed by many other perceptive people, brings attention to the reality that the foods we eat influence our physical and mental health, and they can also influence our actions. If food is deficient in light, we have less light to work with.

Living Spirit—One of Rudolf Steiner's observations was that an essential spiritual requirement of the modern age is to be aware of the increasingly powerful influence of regressive, materialistic impulses, which tend to numb or deaden the living spirit. Such awareness, born of observation, reflection, and engagement, is an element of deep agroecology.

Steiner cautioned that if, for example, mechanical strategies of efficiency were imposed upon beehives, they would wither and fail. With the widespread use of chemicals and mechanistic processes such as interrupting brood production, artificial insemination of queens, and clipping queens' wings, the natural masterwork of the hive has been tamed into a weakened industrial state. The loss of bees and other pollinators has been recognized as a steadily unfolding global disaster with mechanistic, materialistic causes.

Long Term—A 2009 paper from The Land Institute in Salina, Kansas, demonstrated vision and careful long-term thinking, crucial elements of agroecology and deep agroecology. Drawing from the thinking of a wide coalition of sustainable farm organizations, the paper, titled "50 Year Land Bill," set out a vision for gradual systemic change in agriculture based on clean, sustainable practices backed by scientific feasibility. While 50 years does not span the native concept of seven generations, it does in this case give researchers and policy makers a thoughtful example of a long-term perspective.

Land Trust—Land ownership has always been a monumental challenge, especially for young people wanting a career in farming. Land speculators have driven the price of arable land out of the reach of most young people and made maintaining ownership difficult. Land near cities, where market opportunities are greatest for starting farmers, is often the most expensive. Community and agrarian land trusts have established model pathways that are in keeping with the ideals of agroecology and deep agroecology. Land trusts are nonprofit organizations, often started by community members to protect specific resources, such as wildlife habitat, farmland, or water resources, that are at risk from commercial pressures, development, or debilitating damage of some kind. These trusts range in size and capacity from all-volunteer local groups to large national organizations with offices in multiple states.

Land trusts can help farmers access affordable farmland by buying farmland at its agricultural value and then making it available to qualified farmers with affordable, long-term leases. There are many other variations on how people can partner with land trusts. They can assure that farmers have access to farmland and that the farmland remains open and productive over the long-term to provide sustenance for people.

Purpose Trust—The Food and Environment Reporting Network (FERN) published an instructive story in 2018 about a successful organic produce distributor in the Pacific Northwest that sold its business through a Sustainable Food and Agriculture Perpetual Purpose Trust, which is designed to last forever.

This approach addresses what FERN called "the paradox of the organic food industry." To wit, small companies that are established as alternatives to mainstream food brands become popular, and eventually get sold—often to Big Food companies.

Through the *purpose trust* structure, the pressure of the typical business scenario (the need to maximize short-term quarterly profits) is removed. Instead, in this case the organic produce distributor, Organically Grown Co., set out to maximize *purpose* by creating long-term returns to investors who were mission-aligned and then sharing the balance of profits with stakeholders, including farmers, coworkers, customers, and community. Although the purpose trust concept is new in the US, it has been used in Europe.

Honor and Respect—As expressed by one Abenaki elder from Vermont, Wolf Song: "To honor and respect means to think of the land, the water, and plants and animals who live here as having a right equal to our own to be here. We are not the supreme and all-knowing beings, living at the top of the pinnacle of evolution, but in fact we are members of the Sacred Hoop of life, along with the trees and rocks, the coyotes and the eagle, and fish and toads, that each fulfills its purpose. They each perform their given task in the sacred hoop, and we have one, too."

Animal Relatives—Each year more than nine billion animals go to slaughterhouses in the US to be killed, processed, and packaged into the beef, pork, lamb, and chicken that eventually find their way onto our dinner plates. It is an industrial process on a staggeringly vast scale, and it has some fundamental problems.

Our relationship with our animal relatives constitutes a leading edge in human moral development. As human beings, right now we are engaging in that relationship in a troubling manner. The experience the animals endure in mass, industrial confinement not only has economic, environmental, health, and social effects but also moral ramifications. Most Americans—96 percent of us—eat meat of one kind or another. Questions about where our meat came from, how the animals were treated when alive, and how they were killed and prepared for our tables are fundamental. They matter a lot, and in a lot of ways.

Every being on Earth must kill to eat, whether the killing is an insect, a blade of grass, a vegetable plant, a seed, a bird, a butterfly, a bacteria, or a complex mammal. What is the philosophical basis by which human beings decide the nature of their relationship with the creatures they kill and eat? The evolving direction of agroecology and deep agroecology is to acknowledge the shadow side of the animal-human food chain, to recognize how fundamental the quality of respect is in these relationships, and to strive to respond with integrity and respect.

From the stockyard to those with meat in their mouths, everyone involved has a responsibility to face the shadow and to weigh the considerations.

Animal Factories—Organic farmers ostensibly have to accommodate animals' natural behaviors, but relevant USDA Organic standards have been weakened in recent years as a consequence of industry lobbying. By now we have animal factories with as many as 15,000 cows on what are called "organic farms." Big ag is pushing, in many cases distorting, organic standards to make this possible. Now that transnational corporations have invested in organics, they angle to use that label for marketing purposes with as little encumbrance as possible, in terms of their bottom line.

One of the most glaring examples of paradoxical contrast between economic and ecological outcomes is the CAFO (concentrated animal feeding operation) system for meat production.

While the number of animals fated to pass through industrial processes has continued to grow in recent decades, the number of independent family farmers who care for them has continued to decline. High-efficiency corporate, franchised mechanical processes and confinement strategies optimize profit. But the animals are relegated to "units of production." The population of human beings in our rural regions in the heartland of America has been decimated as farmers have steadily fallen victim to vertical integration and to the relentless economic demands of corporate bottom lines.

Through intensive focus on efficiency and profit, large operations have spawned coldly rational mechanistic systems that are well suited to machines but not to living beings such as cows, pigs, lambs, chickens, and turkeys. CAFOs bring into focus philosophical questions at the heart of our moral evolution as human beings living in relationship with animal beings on a finite planet with a fragile environment.

Changing Relationships—According to research published in the journal *Climate Policy* in late 2018, at the present rate, cattle and other farmed animals will be responsible for half of the world's greenhouse gas emissions by 2030. The researchers concluded that for a livable planet, it's vital that we change our relationship with meat, especially with red meat, because production is having a profoundly negative impact on the stability of Earth's climate.

For ethical, environmental, and health reasons, many people are either reducing or eliminating meat from their diets. According to a 2019 report from the market research firm Mintel, consumers are increasingly seeking food and drink innovations that are sustainable and healthy. There is a long-term trend of people reducing meat consumption or switching altogether to vegetarian or vegan diets, a trend that began surging in 2015, according to Schieber Research.

We Have Responsibilities—As animal advocates point out, we have been in relation with farmed animals for millennia, yet animal life does not exist solely to fulfill human appetites. The issues are not just animal rights but also our human responsibility to our animal relatives.

If industrial food-production corporations continue to regard animals as just dumb commodities—units of production to be fattened with genetically modified grains grown in oceans of glyphosate and then pumped up beyond natural reason with hormones and antibiotics—and if we continue to hand them our food money to perpetuate the system, then can we say we are in a right and respectful relationship with farmed animals?

Sacred Ground—During a phone interview for this book, Brooke Medicine Eagle told me about Sacred Ground International, a 3,500-acre nonprofit ranch in Pryor, Montana, on the Crow Reservation. Medicine Eagle is a singer, songwriter, teacher, and earthkeeper. Her longtime friend, Tanah Whitemore, is the eco-rancher who has guided the ranch into a radiant state of environmental health. Having grown up on a ranch that, years ago, became part of Sacred Ground, this is Medicine Eagle's home territory. She feels admiration and appreciation for what Sacred Ground has been accomplishing and modeling for others, and grateful to be a part of it.

When Tanah first inherited the ranch, the land was ravaged from drought and overgrazing. Sheep were thick for mile after mile and the outbuildings and equipment in need of renewal. As she set to work, Tanah was given five buffalo. From these, a herd began to grow. Initial schemes to fence the growing herd and move them systematically from pasture to pasture soon gave way to the reality the buffalo did not wish to be restricted. When they wanted to go somewhere, they would power through fences.

Eventually over time, following their own instincts, the buffalo themselves managed the land. "They knew where to go and how to be," Medicine Eagle said. "Pasture land started coming back. They established buffalo wallows, and pretty soon the water collecting in the wallows created a seep." The seep in turn magnetized underground water. Soon several new springs began flowing on the land. Healthy native grasses and unusual plants with healing attributes began coming back. The land was restored to radiance.

Once there were millions and millions of buffalo roaming across the heart of North America. "They bring spirit energy where they go," Medicine Eagle said. "They are the Giveaway Animal. They give the people all they need."

As the buffalo herd prospered at the ranch, gradually there arose an understanding that it was time to harvest some of the buffalo for meat and hides. After a long stretch of contemplation and planning, Sacred Ground established the honorable harvest.

Honorable Harvest—Sacred Ground sets up their honorable harvest like this: Hunters apply. If accepted, they get an orientation. The hunters cleanse themselves and prepare in ceremony, then offer up prayer requests for an animal to offer itself for the people. They then go out on the land, find the herd, sit and wait nearby on an overlook. Time passes.

"But before long," Medicine Eagle explained, "one buffalo will come out of the herd and stand near the hunters.

When the buffalo presents itself, it will look all around, getting a 360-degree remembrance of its surroundings. A radiant light comes out of them. You see it. It's radiant. The buffalo that is offering itself will stand there for a while in this light. But the hunter can't take a shot until he can shoot behind the head in the neck. So the hunters wait.

"Eventually, the buffalo turns, stands, and opens its neck for the shot. By that time most everyone is crying. They understand that the buffalo is giving itself to them. But it's time. The shot is fired. The buffalo drops. But the herd is hardly disturbed. After a minute or so the buffalo that are direct family relations of the Giveaway, come over to the sacrificed buffalo and stand around in deep silence for a while. Then silently they turn and go back among the herd. The hunters come forward then to offer tobacco in thanksgiving, and to recover the Giveaway."

"By this time," Medicine Eagle said, "if you are a hunter who wanted meat for his family, you know you are related to the buffalo as well. They are part of your family, too. They are giving to you. All they ask in return is caring and respect for their sacrifice. That's what I call Sacred Ranching or Sacred Agroecology, recognizing the life of everything and then giving thanks and respect."

Pulling Forces—I asked Severine T. Fleming what she thought deep agroecology might be about. She's a farmer and an activist, cofounder of Agrarian Trust and director of The Greenhorns, a grassroots organization with the mission to recruit, promote, and support the rising generation of farmers.

"Toward deep agroecology," she said, "there's a practice that can be aspired to. It has to do with sensing, sensing toward the next state of the particular climate that you are in. There's a certain amount of climate destiny that we are bound into, and that we must attune to. How does nature learn and adapt to the stimulus of the atmosphere and planetary conditions? That's what I get out of deep agroecology."

Severine continued: "I think the indigenous world view is that the Earth is animate: full of spirit, and spirit with will. Every creature, every plant, is self-willed. That's part of the profound wisdom of life on Earth. This distributed volition is throughout the system. It not just our will, our dominion, but us in relationship.

"One of the truths about agriculture has to do with forces. In the beginning, we humans had an idea about engaging the plants for food with agriculture. The plants of course also had ideas about life. And then there are the particular circumstances that a given farmer faces, the various constraints.

"So there are three pulling forces. The pulling force of us humans became extreme, with our powerful impacts on the land, water, and so forth. But now the force of the climate and the impact of the degraded Earth are pulling even more strongly. What can emerge, what must emerge, is sensing the reaction of the third pole. What do the plants want? What's their innate nature? What are their impulses? Their next moves? We must be open and attuned to that."

Ceremony—Through ceremony, we human beings join our experience of land and life with the subtle, ephemeral realm of light. In manifold ways, in cultures around the whole world, the material and spiritual are intentionally woven together with song, dance, contemplation, and sacred oration. Especially for farms and food, every culture has had a way of expressing thanksgiving and petitioning for continued bounty. The ceremonial forms of the world are vital social, cultural, and energetic elements of deep agroecology.

In a phone conversation for this book, biodynamic farmer and consultant Matias Baker shared what he has learned. "Ceremony is to create an inner mood that we can then carry out into the world. Each time we direct our will intentionally toward a common good or toward spiritual benefactors through ceremony," he said, "we make it possible for them in turn to congregate in their own way in relationship."

"The key word is renewal," Matias said. "That's what ceremony can help bring. The renewal process begins in the transformation of our own soul faculties, thinking and willing. When we do ceremony, we establish a state of grace, a creative force that showers into the community and into the impulse of the work. In this way we are better enabled to see how to proceed on the farm and in life."

Sharing—Thanks to an introduction from Chief Tom Porter, I got to spend a day visiting with Lorraine Canoe (1932–2013), Wolf Clan, at her kitchen table at Akwesasne, the Mohawk reservation in northern New York State that extends into Canada. We drank a pot of coffee and talked about the world. She told me of one aspect of their culture, where all the people dance together in a circle. "When we do that," she said, "our feet are tickling and caressing the breast of Mother Earth, to share good feelings with her for all the goodness she gives to us."

Path to Survival—In *Basic Call to Consciousness*, Haudenausenee (Iroquois) native elders wrote: "Brothers and Sisters, we bring to your thoughts and minds that right-minded human beings seek to promote above all else the life of all things. We direct to your minds that peace is not merely the absence of war, but the constant effort to maintain harmonious existence between all peoples, from individual to individual, and between humans and the other beings of this planet. We point out to you that a Spiritual Consciousness is the Path to Survival of Humankind."

Destiny—The ideas of agroecology and deep agroecology arise from a basic recognition that the way we farm will determine the destiny of life on the Earth. Trauger Groh, my coauthor for *Farms of Tomorrow* and *Farms of Tomorrow Revisited*, articulated that idea back in 1986, perhaps earlier. His observation made a profound impact on me, and on many others. I felt then and I feel still that his point is irrefutable, an undeniable reality, a fact of life that we best take on with maximum attention and respect.

As time has gone on, and as agroecology has begun to make an impact around the world, I recognized a need to help educate people about the benefits and promise of agroecology and also to develop the subject further for the general public.

As a concept, deep agroecology endeavors to weave the spiritual realities of planet Earth into direct and balanced relationship with the physical realities. Farmers become the agents, the ambassadors, the sacred emissaries to the Earth on behalf of humanity. Deep agroecology explores the reality of humanity's relationship with the natural world, striving toward eminently practical, healing modalities and systems for being in right spiritual relationship with the land and the animals who sustain our human lives, and with each other.

Deep agroecology goes beyond the concept of treading lightly and intelligently upon farm fields and the rest of the Earth and onward to actively engaging, cultivating, and raising the subtle energies of the farm to such a degree that the farm is established as an oasis of environmental health, radiating a high, clear vibration to the immediate neighborhood, and outward more widely into the world through the food it produces. In this manner, farms serve as a matrix of natural foundations that support physical, moral, community, technological, and spiritual evolution.

Chapter 6

This Is the Holy Land

*"We, the people of this land, have so much to share.
But we still do not have a voice on this land."*

—Larry Littlebird

Winona LaDuke visited Lincoln, Nebraska, in May 2010, planting heirloom seed thoughts in a commanding nexus of industrial agriculture. She had traveled to the state capital from her home on the Ojibwe White Earth Reservation in Minnesota, where she serves as director of two organizations: Native Harvest and Honor the Earth. As the keynote speaker at the fifth annual Chief Standing Bear Breakfast, LaDuke made a number of penetrating remarks.

Standing at the podium in front of about 400 people in the ballroom of the downtown Cornhusker Hotel, she began her oration: "I'm always a little surprised when I hear people say that they are getting on a plane and heading off to the Holy Land. Because the Holy Land is here. This is it right here in America. We are standing right now on Holy Land. My people have known that forever. It's time everyone came to understand it."

As LaDuke uttered the last syllable of her pronouncement about the holy land, I felt the Earth respond, as it sometimes will in a moment of truth. The ground beneath the building expressed a tremble. The subtle shudder continued for 10 seconds or more. It was definite. I felt it. Was it mechanical? No. I knew it was a response from the land. I've experienced that on other occasions. Others seated at my breakfast table that morning felt it too.

"Very often," Winona told the audience, "I heard my father [Sun Bear] say, 'I don't want to hear your philosophy if it won't grow corn.' It took me a long time to understand what he meant. But I get it now. He was on to something important. I know also," she added, "that when you grow your own food it makes you a better human being. It connects you to the land you live upon, and it relieves a certain poverty of spirit."

LaDuke ended her talk with an observation about the great national debate raging on the subject of immigration. "In the circumstances of this there is a cruel irony," she said. "Most of the people who are intended to be excluded from this land by laws come from a genetic lineage that has always been here—family lines that trace back in North America for 10,000 years or longer.

"These relatives," she continued, "are mostly people from Mexico and Central America, and are in many cases farmworkers: people who labor in the fields to grow our grains and vegetables, or who toil like machines in the vast confined animal feeding operations (CAFOs) and slaughterhouses that yield our chicken, beef, and pork. Whether we acknowledge and respect these people or not, these are our Ambassadors to the Holy Land. They touch the Earth on our behalf. They raise up the food that we eat. They are human beings, too."

CHORUS OF VOICES

With this chapter I am striving to weave a nonlinear web of information out of a chorus of experiences and voices. My hope is that the overall song created by this chorus will be heard by the people of all the cultures that have come on to this land over the last 500-plus years. There is much to be gained.

If the concepts of deep agroecology outlined in this book seem impossibly idealistic and unrealistic to readers, then in this chapter I want to present an argument that while deep agroecology is indeed idealistic, the vision is necessary and attainable. The pathway to realization of the vision first leads to the native roots on this land. For over five long centuries here have been systematic, ongoing, brutal efforts to annihilate those roots, but they are in fact the very elements and attributes that can stabilize us in a time of grave planetary crisis.

One of the contributions I hope to make with this book is to encourage a stronger and more effective bridge of understanding between agroecology and native peoples and knowings—a bridge that is accessible to all people who recognize the fundamental importance of supporting farms and farmers. Native roots can strengthen and help sustain a spiritually evolved culture, a sustainable agricultural technosphere, and a respectful body politic on North America—but only if the roots are acknowledged, respected, embraced, and engaged. Having been on this land the longest and most respectfully, native people hold a tradition of knowings that can inform essential aspects of our culture, as well as agriculture specifically.

Native nations are not homogenous but rather expressive of a wide array of cultural and earthkeeping traditions. One mutual understanding, as I've been able to grasp it, is the shared idea that we human beings have a responsibility to take care of each other and the Earth. That's considered to be an *original instruction*. The countless, beautiful ways in which the instruction is honored and given expression in native cultures brings a needed element of poetry to teachings of land and life. Toward that end, this chapter is a pastiche of experiences and voices arising from the Holy Land. It's not a linear scientific exposition but rather a grouping of stories. Listen.

Original Instructions—I lived near Manitonquat (1929–2018) for 20 years in the Monadnock region of New Hampshire. Over time I became one of his many friends. Manitonquat (a.k.a. Medicine Story) was a bard, someone who—with his voice, his trained acting skill, and his drum—could transport audiences into dominions of dramatic imagination and received wisdom.

For many years Manitonquat served as Keeper of the Lore for the Assonet Band of the Wampanoag Nation in southeast Massachusetts. The Wampanoags were the people who welcomed the Pilgrims and showed them how to grow corn, beans, and squash. They have a great number of wonderful stories, and Manitonquat had the voice and dramatic skill to tell the tales with memorable beauty and power.

When I interviewed Manitonquat formally in the late 1980s, he spoke of natural law: "Native people refer to the Original Instructions often in speech and prayer, but rarely attempt to say exactly what they are. They are not like the Ten Commandments carved in stone. They are not ideas. They are reality. They are natural law. They are the way thing are—the operational manual for a working Creation—and they cannot be totally understood in words. They must be experienced. The Original

Instructions are not imposed by human minds on the world. They are of the living spirit. Other creatures follow them instinctively, and they are communicated to humankind through the heart, through feelings of beauty and love."

"The Original Instructions," he continued, "urge us to find our place in the cosmos, to know our true nature and our goal in existence. There must be a response—not an intellectual answer—but a felt understanding of the nature of this existence, of its purpose and of our part in that purpose. That is the reason for the spiritual quests, the religions, the rituals, the searches, pilgrimages, meditations, and all the mystic disciplines of humankind. Something in our consciousness is just not satisfied with only eating, sleeping, creating, and reproducing. Something in us wants to know what it's all about and how we fit into it."

Not Easily Described—Back in the early 1990s, I sat in conversation with Penobscot Grandmother Eunice Baumann-Nelson, PhD, at her home on Indian Island, across the river from Old Town, Maine. I was interviewing her for my book *Profiles in Wisdom*. She told me: "The world of the Native American, spiritual and otherwise, is not to be understood by assuming that it can be described easily in the English language, and in religious terms. What we now think of as spirituality was not a religion in the commonly accepted definition of the word. It was their way of life, which is to say that it permeated their lives to such an extent as to be inseparable from everyday living.... Manitou was not a supreme being, but rather a way of referring to the cosmic, mysterious power existing everywhere in nature."

Sacred Hoop—Native peoples indigenous to the Americas have likewise long appreciated a foundational truth of connection or relationship and held that knowing in the forefront as they refined a culture and an agriculture particular to this place, North America, over 12,000 years or more. Rather than using abstract intellectual constructs such as quantum field theory or general relativity, native knowings are conveyed in elegant, tangible metaphors, such as the teaching of the Sacred Hoop (Circle of Life) or the teaching that we have a fundamental responsibility to take care of the Earth, for she is our mother (*Tierra Madre, Pachamama*).

All My Relations—The foundational realization of wholeness and interconnectedness has long been held in many native communities. By way of example, the Lakota people of the Great Plains have a common expression in their language, *Mitákuye Oyás'in*. In English the phrase translates as "all my relations" or "we are all related." It's a simple, direct, sacred speech form for acknowledging the fundamental reality of our relationship and oneness with all life: other people, animals, birds, insects, trees, and plants, and even rocks, rivers, mountains, and valleys. It's all interwoven, all in relation. The phrase expresses a natural, shared world understanding of interconnectedness: All things are related in the *Circle of Life* or the *Sacred Hoop of Life*.

Powwow—Slow Turtle (John Peters, 1930–1997) served as director of the Massachusetts Commission on Indian Affairs for over 20 years. He also held the traditional title of *Massapowah*. In his Wampanoag Algonquin language, *massa* means big and *powau* (powwow) designates the idea of bringing people together. Slow Turtle used to wear a carved turtle necklace, accented with seven beads. The beads were to keep him mindful of the next seven generations of children to come into the world and his responsibility to make a good life possible for them.

When I interviewed him in 1989, Slow Turtle said, "Most of my involvement is with the Indian people and their purpose in life. I think the intentions of my people are entirely different from what mainstream society promotes. We're not here for private gain, but to find a solution to preserve the Earth Mother for all generations to come."

Known but Unspoken—As the Sun approached the solstice in the summer of 2016, my friend Stephen Clarke stopped by my home in Santa Fe, New Mexico, to visit. He sat with me at the picnic table by our garden. In the afternoon light, we talked. Stephen spun out for me the tale of his recent journey up onto the Colorado Plateau near the Lukachukai Mountains, close by the imaginary straight line that legally, if not naturally, separates Arizona and New Mexico. Among many elements, this part of the Navajo Reservation is a place of high elevation, white reeds, rich farmland, uranium, tangled history, and big sky.

An astute observer of matters physical and metaphysical, and also the former proprietor and master mechanic at Mozart's Garage BMW and Mercedes shop in Santa Fe, Stephen made his journey to sit with his Navajo friends as part of a weeklong *Nadáá* healing ceremony.

In telling the tale of his visit to Lukachukai, he mentioned how the community of people came together in hard work and good fellowship to abide with one another over the course of a week and to make ceremony expressing timeless ways and courtesies, all woven together within a group energy field of respect and humor many times larger than themselves.

"As I'm able to grasp it, native people know how to cooperate in community," he told me. "It's silent, it's unspoken, but it is known and known implicitly by everyone....

Native people know already that the spirit lives not only in the land, but also within in their relationships with it and with one another. As part of their way, for thousands of years they have had the understanding of spirit life on a practical level."

"There's a western axiom that 'the map is not the territory,'" Stephen told me, "but as I see it that's not so in traditional native contexts. The land itself is the map, and that land map is also indivisibly the territory wherein life unfolds. Physicality and spirituality are not separated by concepts or perceptions, to be worshiped in a metaphysical superstructure high off the ground, but are appreciated as one interpenetrating and mutually revealing reality. Native people have the land as a source of spirituality and as the reference point for their spiritual lives. As I've come to appreciate it, their relationship to the spiritual world is very concrete and not esoteric."

As Stephen related, his Navajo relatives in Lukachukai—with grace and spiritual intelligence, and via basic interactions with each other and nature—demonstrated their appreciation of community and spiritual realities. It's their way. And their way is part of the strength of the rootstock: the native spiritual, cultural, and agricultural knowings that have been cultivated and developed in North America for many thousands of years.

Rootstock—A rootstock is part of a plant, often an underground part, from which new above-ground growth can be produced. Grafting refers to the process by which a plant, sometimes just a stump with an established root system, serves as the base onto which cuttings (scions) from another plant are joined. Grafting generally ensures a strong, healthy, and productive crown, arising from a mature root system. It's also an apt metaphor.

The cultural ways that have been in recent centuries arriving in North America from Europe, Africa, Asia, and the Global South have never been deliberately joined with the rootstock. Instead, there has been a concerted, systematic, violent, and tragic attempt to annihilate the rootstock of native peoples and wisdom ways through protracted campaigns of genocide, wholesale landgrabbing, and systematic treaty violations. That pattern has generated a massive energy field of karma, as yet unreckoned.

Finding Our Home—A successful, healthy, conscious grafting of the world's multitude of cultural and spiritual ways to the rootstock of Turtle Island (North America) would, I reckon, yield a harvest of goodness. The possibilities are not just philosophical but altogether practical and potentially beautiful. Considering the status of climate upheaval in the Americas and around the world, they're also urgent. As we are rocked by repeated waves of tumultuous weather unleashed by climate change and sharp shifts in politics, economics, and society, something durable is called for—something strong, wise, rooted in the land, waiting at last to find a home in our souls, and for our souls to finally, respectfully, find a home on this land.

The core native knowings that have been part of culture and agriculture on this land for millennia can enhance our capacity to respond adroitly to the dissolving and shattering forces aroused in our era. Now, in an era of pervasive change, it's both an auspicious and a decisive time for the individuals, groups, states, and nations of North America to face the historic and contemporary reality by learning more deeply about, respecting actively, and engaging more constructively with the cultural and agricultural rootstock of the land we now share.

Traditional Ecological Knowledge—In recent years researchers have begun to pay attention to traditional ecological knowledge, TEK, or native knowings, to enrich their understanding of the natural world. In academic terms TEK is described as deep knowledge of a place that has been discovered and passed on by those who have adapted to it over thousands of years. Native peoples have depended on this knowledge for their survival over the millennia. As climate change intensifies and more and more species of plants and animals go extinct, TEK often offers meaningful insight into attaining right relationship and balance.

Reservations—The clarity and penetrating insight of many native teachings and native lineage holders is remarkable, and in so many ways precisely what the Americas need now. But at the same time, life in native communities is often harsh and unhealthy. The rate of poverty on US reservations is close to 30 percent. Drug and alcohol abuse are common. While the average life expectancy for Native Americans has improved in recent decades, the average still trails that of other Americans by almost five years. There are a great many environmental, health, and social challenges to be overcome.

Studies have concluded that major dietary issues in indigenous communities are linked to increasing dependence on highly processed foods, mainly consisting of white flour, lard, and sugar, which can make up to 85 percent of the diet in native communities that have been forced away from more nutritious traditional foods such as fish, wild game, and berries. Consequently, there is an epidemic of lifestyle disease occurring among indigenous peoples, diseases such as type 2 diabetes mellitus, cardiovascular disease, hypertension, autoimmune disease, and obesity. While these diseases are also increasing in the larger populations of North America, they are more prevalent in indigenous populations.

Since 2013, the First Nations Development Institute has been actively organizing Food Sovereignty Summits, annual forums for sharing and collaboration to build healthy food systems within Native American communities. Those summits are making a positive difference.

Unharnessed Knowledge—Lynn Ghel, PhD, offers a bridge of understanding in her 2017 book, *Claiming Anishinaabe: Decolonizing the Human Spirit.* Gehl is an Algonquin Anishinaabe-kwe, an advocate, artist, and author. She writes, "Anishinaabe philosophers of the Midewiwin were masters in understanding the importance of both the heart and mind as repositories of knowledge. They knew that reason alone was insufficient in shaping a person toward the good life. As such, our systems of knowing were wholistic, meaning they served to shape and guide a person's mind and heart and body."

To convey what she learned about the difference between indigenous knowledge and scientific positivism, she developed a model called "unharnessed knowledge." While scientific positivism is narrow and focused, indigenous knowledge is broader and values beliefs, song, ritual, storytelling, community, and relationships. "Once I accepted heart knowledge as a legitimate way of coming to know," she writes, "I began to listen, feel and think more carefully."

It's Pretty Simple—When poet and educator Beata Tsosie-Peña of Santa Clara Pueblo spoke at the 2017 Mountain West Seed Summit in Santa Fe, she made a telling point. A permaculture specialist and a member of Tewa Women United, she said, "Violence done to our Mother Earth is the same as the violence done to girls and women. Can we de-colonize the thought that the earth is a commodity? The original instructions have to do with loving and caring for each other. It's pretty simple. Our survival is now entwined together."

Basic Understandings—The root cultural and agricultural knowings of North America constitute basic understandings for long-term survival on this land. The knowings have been gained not over mere centuries but over many thousands of years. In light of our present circumstances, these knowings are both relevant and essential.

For some time healthy natural grafting processes have been progressing in the array of agroecological movements toward clean, wholesome land, water, and food. These initiatives include good food, slow food, organic food, food justice, food sovereignty, and a variety of First Nations organizations, including the Traditional Native American Farmers Association, the Native American Food Sovereignty Alliance, and the 2018 launch of the Native American Agriculture Fund. Such initiatives are positive and promising and need ongoing support to meaningfully impact food systems.

The structure of the dominant food system has origins that extend back through history at least to genocide of native people and theft of their land, to slavery on farms and plantations, to the corporate forces that have driven hundreds of thousands of farm families off the land, to our current wholesale dependence upon and exploitation of farmworkers. All that has to be faced, reckoned with, and resolved or it remains toxic—toxic in a turbulent era.

Key to Survival—On an August evening in 2009, in the garden of the late sculptor Alan Houser, I met recording artist and teacher of peace Joanne Shenandoah, Oneida Nation, and her husband, author and orator Doug George-Kanentiio, Mohawk. They had come to contribute gifts of song and speech to benefit a native charity. The Oneida and Mohawk peoples are part of the Iroquois Confederacy of Six Nations, known rightly as Haudenosaunee (hô-den´ə-shô´nē).

As the Sun began to set, Shenandoah took the microphone, faced south, centered herself, and gave voice to her enthralling composition, *Prophecy Song*: "We are now reminded to be aware of our place upon this earth, and to fulfill our obligations to ourselves, our families, our nations, the natural world, the Creator...."

Having performed and taught widely in the world, Shenandoah has entitled one of her lectures "Living for the Seventh Generation and Beyond." In it, she explains that "the key to survival will be the ability to live within sustainable societies which secure balance between basic human resource needs and the rights of other species. The Iroquois have a constitutional obligation to do nothing which qualifies the rights of the unborn to clean water, fertile land, and clear skies. To achieve this, the Iroquois incorporate the rights of others from the earth to insects, animals, plants and trees. All have legal standing which must be respected."

Voice of the Grandmothers—As a model to help inform emerging new systems, consider the Haudenosaunee traditions as expressed by Barbara Alice Mann in her book *Iroquoian Women: The Gantowisas*. Dr. Mann is a humanities scholar at University of Toledo. She is also a member of the Seneca Nation, Bear Clan, part of the Iroquois League. In her book she explains that "Gantowisas" is the word for clan mothers, government women, indispensable women. She reports that in the 1700s when invading troops began incursions into Iroquois territory, the fields tended by native women "covered acreage as far as the eye could see, with high crop yields." She cites abundant evidence to back up her statement. From these women farmers, the colonial Europeans adopted the staple crops that now help sustain the world: corn, beans, squash, potatoes.

Dr. Mann points out that the economic principles of the Iroquois differ significantly from Western ideals. Iroquois economic theory starts from the premise of plenty, as opposed to the European premise of scarcity. Further, Iroquois economics was a spiritual system. "If materialism underpins capitalism," she writes, "spirituality is the core of Iroquoian communalism... The Iroquoian Plenty Way did not depend on private property rights, but on the understanding that women are the stewards, The Keepers of Mother Earth, not her grasping overlords. What they hold is a sacred trust, not an exploitative right."

Four Sacred Medicines—As held in the millennia-old knowings of Turtle Island (North America), tobacco is appreciated as the first plant that Creator gave to the human beings. Part of the nightshade family, tobacco has a special role. It is chief among the plants—the most significant medicine. Three other plants, sage, cedar, and sweetgrass, join tobacco to make four sacred medicines, but tobacco is regarded by many as primary.

Having had opportunities to be with and to learn from many native teachers over the last four decades, I've encountered some of the basic spiritual understandings about tobacco. Because tobacco is understood to play such a key role in the natural world and in human life, and because the related derangement and collapse of the world's bee colonies is so important to our survival, the subject merits both physical and metaphysical study.

As held in the teachings I received over the years, tobacco was given to human beings to help people communicate with the spirit world, a world present in every animal, plant, and mineral being. Powerful in a subtle manner beyond contemporary appreciation when used knowingly and respectfully, tobacco can help open a portal allowing communication to take place in a safe, conscious, and wholesome manner. There's a lot to learn in just that simple facet of the tobacco teachings, and it's good to have an experienced teacher. Traditional people say, "always through tobacco." Tobacco is always first, used as an offering for most everything and in every ceremony.

Synthetic Tobacco—In bleakly enormous numbers, billions of bees, birds, and bats continue to perish. These massive, mysterious pollinator exterminations are steadily stinging our food supply and the whole of the natural world. One out of every three bites of food we consume is directly linked to pollinators. Thus, as the bees go, so go we. While the precise cause of bee colony collapse is still argued, clues continue to emerge. Among the chief suspects is the widespread use of a reductionist, synthetic form of tobacco as an agricultural or backyard insecticide.

As for beekeepers, they are increasingly convinced that an underlying cause of this global death plague is a family of insecticides called *neonicotinoids*. They are chemicals that mimic the form and function of nicotine, the naturally occurring alkaloid in tobacco. In synthetic, chemical form, the neonicotinoids are sprayed on seeds or crops to keep them clear of insects. The neonicotinoids, in combination with a "chemical soup" of other substances, are widely believed to be a major player in the massive bee die-off being described collectively as Colony Collapse Disorder (CCD).

As chief of the plant realm, tobacco can be employed for great good or great harm. This has been understood for generations. In this context, the widespread commercial use of manufactured, synthetic tobacco—a substance reduced to a base material form—appears as a matter of agricultural and spiritual significance.

Flower of Your Heart—As a young man in the 1980s, Brant Secunda was invited into the rich cultural and agricultural tradition of *Los Huicholes*, the Huichol Indians of Mexico's Sierra Madre mountains. There he trained for many years before helping to carry the traditional teachings out into the wider world, which is what he was doing when I met him in the early 1990s. He established the Dance of the Deer Foundation to help share the teachings more widely through seminars and publications. The June

2018 newsletter from his Dance of the Deer Foundation related one of those teachings. According to the Huichol, our hearts are a mirror of the universe that surrounds us. Through spiritual practice, we can learn to perceive this mirror more clearly.

"The simple act of connecting with a mountain, a river or the ocean in this way can help us to gain nuggets of cosmic wisdom, to better understand the underlying interconnectedness that ties everything together," the newsletter relates. "As we progress on the shamanic path, we eventually begin to understand that everything external is also within and vice versa. With this perspective, we realize that our effects on our environment have an intrinsic effect on our own heart. And the work we do to purify, empower and brighten our heart has a direct effect on everything around us. The Huichol say, 'Open the *Tutu* (the flower of your heart). Nourish your heart; feed it with love and water it with light so that it can blossom beautifully for the entire universe to enjoy.'"

Three Sisters—In her book *Braiding Sweetgrass*, author Robin Wall Kimmerer observes that the Three Sisters (corn, beans, and squash) can be regarded as a metaphor for the emerging relationship between Western science and indigenous knowledge. She sees corn as representing traditional knowings, the stalk standing tall, which can guide upward the helix-twining tendrils of the beans, symbolic of science. In a healing picture drawn from her imagination, she sees this relationship surrounded by the ethical environment characterized by the squash plants. "I envision a time," Kimmerer writes, "when the intellectual monoculture of science will be replaced with a polyculture of complementary knowledges."

Explicit Consideration—The UN's Intergovernmental Science-Policy Platform on Biodiversity and Ecosystem Services (ISPPBES) published a kick-in-the-gut report (2019) about extinction of our local life-support system, Earth. Their report—based on the work of 450 researchers from around the world and 15,000 scientific and government reports—warned of immediate, grave danger.

Sir Robert Watson, who served as chair of the study, said, "The overwhelming evidence ... from a wide range of different fields of knowledge, presents an ominous picture. The health of ecosystems on which we and all other species depend is deteriorating more rapidly than ever. We are eroding the very foundations of our economies, livelihoods, food security, health and quality of life worldwide."

Deep in the report, among the "key" recommendations about ways to respond to the challenges of these conditions was a brief section under the heading "Indigenous Peoples, Local Communities and Nature."

Here's a key excerpt: "Regional and global scenarios currently lack, and would benefit from, an explicit consideration of the views, perspectives, and rights of Indigenous Peoples and local communities, their knowledge and understanding of large regions and ecosystems, and their desired future development pathways."

We Know Something—"We cannot order or demand anyone to do anything. We can only tell you what we know, and hope and pray that you will listen," Algonquin Grandfather William Commanda said on September 24, 1995. I was with him as he led a prayer walk through Memphis, Tennessee, and I made formal note of his words so they could be included in my online journal about the epic walk, *Odyssey of the 8th Fire*.

Grandfather Commanda said: "We native people know something. After having lived here on this land for many, many thousands of years, we have learned some things. We don't know it all, but we do know something. Right now we have a choice, but that choice is very hard. But we must make that choice now so that our children will have the possibility of the life that we have had. We love you, we love you all, and we are depending on you to help us make life possible for our children and for your children."

Chapter 7

Tierra Viva

"There is practically no field of human endeavor that does not relate to agriculture in some way. Seen from whatever perspective you choose, agriculture touches on every single aspect of human life."

—Rudolf Steiner

I was going to title this chapter "The Intersection of Main Street, *Camino Real*, and the Red Road," but that was too cumbersome and made no explicit provision for the Asian, African, and other multicultural ways that have streamed together with everyone and everything on North America. We are whirling about in a confluence of cultural, environmental, health, and community matters—matters that all depend inevitably on our farms and food. These matters are critical to our lives, to the lives of our children, and to the lives of our children's children, unto seven generations or more. There's no responsible way to dodge that.

Eventually for this chapter I settled on *Tierra Viva*. That was the name of the 2016 Biodynamic Association conference in Santa Fe, New Mexico. *Tierra viva* means "living earth," and the conference focused on how we human beings draw our sustenance by farming the living earth and how we might do that more respectfully and successfully.

Farms and food are key places where—physically and metaphysically—the multitude of cultures that have streamed onto North America from around the world have an essential and passionately shared interest. We will find our ways forward on the living earth by connecting respectfully with the ancient wisdom teachings of this Turtle Island continent and rooting in this the congregation of cultural influences that have been transplanted here, along with the brilliant, emerging Seventh Generation technology streams arising from ethical science.

This chapter is an exploration of some of those ways forward as they are arising in thoughts and deeds.

Gaia Hypothesis—In antiquity, many cultures around the globe, and certainly on North America, appreciated the Earth as a living being. In our era the *Gaia hypothesis* has reintroduced the concept to technological cultures. Initially developed by chemist James Lovelock and microbiologist Lynn Margulis in the 1970s, the theory has gained wide currency. It observes that living organisms interact with their inorganic surroundings to form a complex, self-regulating synergistic system that helps maintain the conditions necessary for life on Earth. These planetary systems have evolved together—much as the organs of any human being's body have developed together to make a whole.

Thus, our home planet can rightly be thought of as a being, the earth being. In Greek mythology, primordial, full-figured Gaia is one of the original Goddesses of Olympus, characterized as the very Spirit of the Earth. Gaia is Mother Earth, the mother of all life. The Gaia hypothesis is a helpful way of understanding life on our planet and an element of deep agroecology. Earth has spirit and soul. With this our human spirit and soul abides. It's essential that respect permeate this matrix of relationship.

Living Earth—During a plenary session at Tierra Viva, Biodynamic Association codirector Thea Maria Carlson stepped to the podium to address the 500 or so conference participants. She said, "A widespread problem is people not seeing the earth as a living being. Thus, our conference theme, Tierra Viva."

The conference was a landmark moment for the Biodynamic Association, a chance to explore more fully, and to root more deeply, in the Americas. The biodynamic impulse came to North America from Europe many decades ago, as have so many other cultural elements. The staff, board, and members of the association have defined biodynamics as "a holistic, ecological, and ethical approach to farming, gardening, food, and nutrition." At the Tierra Viva conference, the biodynamic movement entered intentionally into a community collaboration with indigenous relatives, a collaboration the organization intends to carry forward.

Recognition—During the Tierra Viva conference, I began to recognize more fully how I might approach the subject of deep agroecology, the topic that Professor Chuck Francis had suggested to me. I saw that I could begin to describe deep agroecology by merging the agrarian knowledge I had gained over the decades with some of the native knowings that I'd come to appreciate over the same span of time. Biodynamics is one way—one pathway—to more intelligently establish a relationship between native knowing and a system initiated in Europe a century ago and brought to America. Biodynamics is open to building connections and relationships among the different ways of knowing.

Matter Never Without Spirit—The initial biodynamic perceptions about nature and preparations to enhance farm and food vitality were indigenous to Europe. Now the perceptions and preparations are global, and they are employed in many different ways in many different geographical and cultural contexts, including North America. The biodynamic impulse is benefiting from being more deliberately grafted with the rootstock of native knowings. Both can be strengthened. This kind of joining was a theme for Tierra Viva.

The biodynamic farming and gardening movement is one of many natural scions available for grafting to North America's cultural and agricultural rootstock. But biodynamics is a particularly propitious domain for fusion. A forerunner of organics, biodynamic agriculture embraces metaphysical realities that organics generally chooses not to consider as factors. In this esoteric manner, biodynamics strives to work intelligently with subtle forces.

When biodynamics was germinating as an agricultural discipline back in the 1920s, teacher Rudolf Steiner encouraged farmers to make use of an ancient principle from the indigenous knowings native to Europe: "*Spirit is never without matter, matter never without spirit.*"

Integrity—While in Santa Fe to teach at Tierra Viva, Hugh Lovel commented that although our culture is changing, most people believe agriculture must fight nature. "We rip up the land and do our best to digest it," Lovel said. "Then we blast it with fertilizers, fight weeds, pests and diseases, and pretty much do whatever it takes to harvest as much as possible of just one thing no matter the overall cost. Killing nature like this lacks integrity. It's no wonder the will to support such stuff is disappearing. The bottom line is foods and medicines grown today are notable for their lack of balance and vitality, to say nothing of their failure to inspire."

Stand Together in Defense of the Sacred—As Joseluis Ortiz of Picuris Pueblo and Placitas Gardens put it when he spoke late Saturday night at Tierra Viva: "It is time for the indigenous communities and the biodynamic community to stand together in defense of the sacred."

Principles and Practices—Robert Karp, at the time co-director of the Biodynamic Association, spoke at Tierra Viva and then again in Santa Fe in May 2018. "Biodynamics is a philosophy with principles and practices," he explained. "The practices are all informed by the principles, and behind all the principles is a philosophy. That philosophy strives to reckon with and interact intelligently with the relationship of the physical world to the spiritual world." To do that, Karp said, "We must learn to think with the heart."

As he sees it, material forces are just one set of influences and are not the only causal factors on land or in life.

Light/etheric forces also stream in and are interacting with all things, animate and nonanimate.

Some familiar, yet invisible, forces are heat, wind, and gravity. Industrial agriculture pays attention to these forces and applies technology. But through the consistent use of mineral fertilizers and allied toxic chemicals, Karp said, industrial farmland is steadily driving the soil into a stone-like condition, with less and less living biota—the trillions of microscopic beings who embody life in healthy soil. Through the approach of most industrial agriculture, the soil and the plants are treated like mechanisms. They need such and such fuel/fertilizer and other conditions, and they will produce X edible result.

Karp said biodynamics is trying to move things the other way, away from material-bound approaches and instead use approaches that work dynamically with subtle forces influencing soil, compost, and plants to provide healthier foods, healthier bodies, and a healthier planet.

A science of life forces, both gross and subtle, biodynamics recognizes the principles at work in nature and strives to develop approaches to agriculture that employ these principles to establish balance. As it continues to develop, biodynamics, like agroecology itself, is more a path of knowledge and development rather than a congregation of techniques.

Cultura de Corazon—Tierra Viva began with a daylong seminar on the theme "Bridging the Americas." Panelists included Matias Baker, Bruno Rodrigues Follador, Osiris Abrego Plata, Eduardo Rincon, Danilo Solano, Thomas Spaulding, and Sarah Weber.

As if participating in an experiment in quantum mechanics, the panelists expressed an entangled wealth of accumulated knowings: various earthkeeper wisdom traditions of the Americas and the agrarian wisdom ways that have streamed onto the continent from Europe, Asia, Africa, and elsewhere around the globe, ways that are finding provincial coherence through the evolving approaches of biodynamic agriculture. It provided a space for people throughout the Americas—South, North, Central, and Caribbean—to meet, connect, and learn from each other.

"This conference is a beginning spark for igniting a flame," said Matias Baker, founder of the Kepher Dynamics biodynamic farming consultancy. Baker declared that our gathering was a seed, helping to further initiatives that would help unite the Americas. "We are in the early stages," he said, "discovering and revealing the mission. We do know the mission will be forever metamorphosing...."

Baker said that a culture of unity cannot unfold solely from intellectual concepts. He spoke of "land guardians" and gave voice to a phrase describing the place where he felt fusion could arise: *El Cultura de Corazon*, a culture of the heart. The phrase *El Cultura de Corazon* gives graspable poetic expression to the concept of deep agro-ecology, which some may regard as abstract, even though it describes something real and urgent.

Condor and Eagle—While listening to Matias Baker give his presentation at Tierra Viva, I was reminded of the teachings of the eagle and the condor, and how the quetzal figures into the relationship.

In 1989 I traveled through Mexico's Yucatan peninsula with Mayan Daykeeper Hunbatz Men and the venerable Don Alejandro Cirilo Perez, Oxlaj, of Guatemala. They were engaging traveling companions, sharing a wealth of insights about the Americas and the traditions that have living roots here reaching many thousands of years into the past, and which hold an intention for the future of a just and spiritually informed culture.

Don Alejandro's name in the Mayan language is *Wakatel Utiw* (Wandering Wolf), a fitting name for a man who has traveled far and wide over the years. He is a 13th-generation Quiche Maya spiritual leader, the leader of the National Council of Elders Mayas, Xinca and Garifuna of Guatemala, and founder and grand elder of the Continental Council of Elders & Spiritual Guides of the Americas. Don Alejandro also served as an official ambassador in the Guatemalan government, representing the rights of indigenous people.

As we traveled together across the Yucatan, Don Alejandro and Hunbatz talked, using their own vernacular, about what other cultures would term yin and yang, the basic polarity at work in the world, and the right and left hemispheres of the brain. All our human capacities—intellectual, emotional, and intuitive—are united in the heart, they said.

Don Alejandro in particular spoke of the ancient teachings about the condor of the south and the eagle of the north. He told me these were understandings held by many of the indigenous cultures in this hemisphere. Specifically, he said, it is appreciated that one day the great sacred birds of South and North America will fly together and symbolize a new, healthier future: merging intelligence and precision with open, feeling hearts.

The eagle and the condor would come together, he said. That coming together will require the aid of the sacred bird of Central America, the resplendently beautiful quetzal, and it will occur in honor of the Sacred Hoop of Life and in respectful service to the next seven generations of our children.

"It is said that when the eagle flies with the condor a lasting peace will reign in the Americas," Don Alejandro explained. "It will spread throughout the world to unite humanity... The teaching is that those of the Center (Central America), with their mystical bird quetzal, will help unite the eagle of the north with the condor of the south. We will meet because we are one, like the fingers of the hand."

A Language of the Heart—In the plaza in front of United Nations headquarters in Manhattan, on August 9, 1995, I heard native elder Alberto Taxo comment on the relationship between the technology-based cultures of the world, which he regards as yang, or masculine eagle in character, and the earth-based, or native, cultures, which he regards as yin, or feminine condor in character. I made note of the whole day and of his oration in particular. "The eagles of the north cannot be fully realized without the condors of the south," he said, "nor can the condors ascend without the eagles."

A member of the Atis (Kichwa) people of the Cotopaxi region in Ecuador, Taxo was there to help mark the first-ever UN-sponsored International Day of the World's Indigenous Peoples. He said he recognizes many provocative social, political, and spiritual currents at work in condor-oriented indigenous nations all around the globe, paralleling currents in the eagle technology-based cultures. Corporate media shuns this knowledge and these parallels, he said. "Consequently, the public remains deprived of information about these crucial parallel developments, and the two sacred cultural currents of North and South America have difficulty finding each other to fly together."

"We the Indigenous People join together in defense of the life of the human species, in defense of the life of our brother animals and the trees, and in defense of the life of Mother Earth, because the life of planet Earth is in danger. Eagle of the north has become so hardened he can no longer fly. The condor comes to resuscitate. A language of the heart can connect us."

Fifth Chamber of the Heart—As the Tierra Viva conference unfolded, Matias Baker cited Rudolf Steiner's ideas about the heart. In a 1922 lecture, "The Human Heart," Steiner indicated that he perceived a nascent fifth chamber of the heart. He spoke of a time when certain changes would take place in the heart, by which gradually a fifth chamber would develop. In this fifth chamber, he said, human beings will have a new organ, etheric in character, evolving to become a spiritual sense organ. This organ, Steiner suggested, would allow human beings to control life forces in a different way than is possible at the moment. "This," Baker said, "can be a force for bridging the Americas."

Evolution—Author Dennis Klocek presented two workshops at the conference. As he explained in various remarks, and also in his book *Sacred Agriculture: The Alchemy of Biodynamics,* one of Rudolf Steiner's foremost contributions was that he recognized the principle of the evolution of consciousness, and he linked that principle to work on the land. From Steiner's point of view, Klocek explained, the evolution of the Earth depends on the evolution of human consciousness. They are not separate.

Elaborating on this, Klocek has written that "the evolution of [human] consciousness requires us to understand that our state of consciousness has an impact on the evolution of the Earth as a spiritual being." He agrees with Rudolf Steiner's observation that for this to happen, farmers must become the agents, the ambassadors, and the priestly emissaries to the Earth on behalf of humanity. This is a role farmers can fulfill only with community support.

Associative Economics—During the Tierra Viva conference, I led a workshop on Community Supported Agriculture (CSA). By now there are upward of 10,000 of these farms in North America giving expression in various ways to CSA principles. The CSA idea has caught on and is maturing. Because economics is a core dimension of CSA farms and of course of any agrarian enterprise, I encouraged workshop participants to look into the concept of associative economics, especially in farm and food matters.

Associative economics is an emergent approach to enterprise that is distinct from capitalism or communism. As author Gary Lamb wrote in *Associative Economics:*

Spiritual Activity for the Common Good, "Associative economics is concerned with and depends on building and sustaining healthy relationships." Indeed, the precepts of associative economics as derived from Rudolf Steiner's indications describe what emerged to become the core mission of CSA farms: economic arrangements that foster fair and healthy interaction among producers, traders, and consumers and where appropriate price, true human needs, greater social equity, and environmental benefits are explicitly addressed in the process.

The efforts of CSA pioneers were aimed at the basic economy of finding ways to free farmers to do the tasks that are right for the farm, for the people, and for the Earth rather than focusing on monetary profit. The key question for a farm that is engaging associative economics, either explicitly or implicitly, is not "How can we make a monetary profit?" Rather, the questions are "What does the farm need? What do the farmers need? What do the shareholders need?" In response to these questions, the community proceeds in its work.

Bridging the Americas—Biodynamics was developed in a particular place on the Earth, Central Europe, following the Steiner lectures in 1924. Then, as with so many other cultural influences, the biodynamic insights came to the Americas. As Bruno Follador referenced when he spoke at Tierra Viva, in the Americas there is a different soul gesture in the land.

"It takes time and care to weave a right relationship in cultural and agricultural ways," Follador said. This establishment of a right relationship is a subject of strong interest for him. He was born and came to maturity in São Paulo, Brazil, one of Earth's largest and most intensely populated cities, and became an agrarian geographer and a consultant in biodynamic agriculture. After many years abroad teaching and researching, Follador and his family have again set roots in Brazil.

In a follow-up phone interview for this book, he explained that with the coming of the Europeans to this hemisphere, what happened in a dominant way, in Latin America, for example, was a fixation on gold, silver, wood, and the monetary wealth these substances represent. He said that obviously not all but many of the people who came to the Americas brought with them a primary intention of exploitation.

"Nature was seen as a great reservoir of natural resources from which things could just be taken, and the cultures that lived here could be annihilated to enable that taking. That's a huge part of the story that we are still living out today."

"We need to learn from each other," Follador continued. "I feel that as a younger continent in some ways we can offer many fresh perspectives, whereas in Europe they may be bound to certain fixed ways. I really feel that in Latin America (and in saying this I don't mean to exclude North America), new insights are arising out of culture and human creativity, always in cooperation with other cultures. We are all children of this one earth."

"When we bring our concepts to nature, especially monetary concepts, we kill it," Follador said. "We need to go on a pathway of the fraternal. The farmers have to become priests, and work to enliven the earth. And all of us need to pay attention to the earth, and to take healing actions. Our participation is needed to heal the earth."

Farmers Are the Great Modern Heroes—When he spoke during Tierra Viva, Bruno Follador cited a passage from Steiner's *Philosophy of Freedom*: "To live in love towards our actions, and to let live in the understanding of the other person's will, is the fundamental maxim of free men."

"When we are truly in the pursuit of agriculture, or in the effort of doing agriculture," he explained, "we are cultivating the land, bringing culture to nature. As many farmers have expressed to me, this is done as a free deed. It's done out of love." He explained that farmers while cultivating the land work a tremendous number of long and hard hours. If you look at the agricultural endeavor from a primarily economic or monetary standpoint, it looks insane. But the farmers are responding from another standpoint, out of their souls. They are responding to a vocational call that they hear, a call that leads them to tend the earth and feed the people.

"In this way," Follador said, "farmers stand as examples of free individuals, because they are enacting their deeds out of love. It is out of this love that the farmer creates a cultural and agricultural reality, which brings the possibility of nourishing the land and the community. In that sense the farmer is free, because he or she could do something else to make more money. But they choose the land for their life."

"We must regard farmers as the great modern heroes, or examples of a human being," Follador told me. "They are constantly in conversation with land. And both the land and the people demand so much of the farmer. But the farmer does what the farmer does out of love. Freely."

Holy Thinking—Patricia Anne Davis presented some of her work at the Tierra Viva farming conference. She is in private practice as a practitioner, diagnostician, and international teacher and consultant of Navajo/Dineh Blessingway ceremonial healing principles. Her work is cross-cultural, intergenerational, inclusive, universal, and practical. As she said while teaching within a circle within a rectangular conference room, "Those who are destroying the planet are outside nature, and they do not recognize how they are part of it. But there are laws of nature, and no one can have power over that."

"We have to stop saying 'yes' to the destruction of the earth," she said. "We need conversations now for our collective survival. Use your holy thinking." The Dineh concept of holy thinking (*ntsahakees*) is understood as whole-brain thinking, spiritual clarity, and awareness of the natural order as reality. She said that for us to fully comprehend the Dineh thinking system, we must experience ourselves as being within *hozho* (natural order), an all-encompassing concept of holiness and wholeness that is affirmative, holistic, within the natural order, based on appreciation of the natural fact that everything is interconnected, and directed toward the application of creative imagination for collective survival.

Chapter 8

What Are Farms For?

"Sacred agriculture is not just the manipulation of resources, but rather a spiritual act. This is an imperative of evolution, as well as an imperative of survival."

—Dennis Klocek

In hundreds of thousands of places in North America and millions of places around the world, individuals, communities, and creative organizations are working dynamically to establish, to restore, and to vitalize clean, healthy, local food systems. Innovations continue to emerge at an encouraging rate. These agrarian initiatives represent promising evolutions in the matrix of our farms and food.

At the same time, industrial-scale systems based on chemicals, machines, and bottom-line economics are continuing to advance far and wide across the land. They produce marketable crops that provide monetary returns for investors, but in many cases they lay waste to the life in the soil, foul our waters with chemicals, imprison millions of farmed animals in harsh, unnatural conditions, and engage human beings in low-wage and often unjust jobs. These practices accelerate ruination of the sources. They undermine our long-term survival. In perpetuating this system, we taint the legacy we are leaving for our children and grandchildren, unto the seventh generation.

Knowledge of these hard realities, combined with recognition of how many millions of people are needed to meet the challenges of our farms and our food, and to establish a legacy of health and beauty, brings me to the rhetorical question posed by agrarian elder Wendell Berry, *What are people for?*

"The great question that hovers over this issue, one that we have dealt with mainly by indifference," Berry wrote in his book by that title, "is the question of what people are *for*. Is their greatest dignity in unemployment? Is the obsolescence of human beings now our social goal? One would conclude so from our attitude toward work, especially the manual work necessary to the long-term preservation of the land, and from our rush toward mechanization, automation, and computerization."

In the main essay Berry answers his own rhetorical question obliquely, noting that there's critical work to be done restoring and caring for our farms, forests, and rural communities. That's indeed work that must be done, and done with the honest pride and the high skill of defenders, protectors, providers, and pathfinders. This is what we need.

If we find within ourselves honest answers to the question *what are people for?* then of wisdom we must ask also, *what are farms for?* Are farms to be massive, remotely owned, industrial-scale, chemical, monoculture land and animal factories employing hourly workers at menial tasks to churn out cheap masses of processed nutritional units? Or could farms be for establishing a far-flung network of agrarian oases radiating environmental, physical, and spiritual health through their landscapes and the clean food and fiber they produce?

Could farms be for serving life not solely as economic engines but rather, in this time of crisis, for serving the essential healing and uplifting of our planet, the people of all the nations, and the animals and plants in the Sacred Hoop—the Circle of Life—who share existence and experience with us on Earth?

Things have unwound a lot since 1985 when Berry raised his soul-arresting question about purpose. So precarious is the state of our world as I write that I'm compelled to state my answer to Berry's question plain and direct, after first responding to a parallel question: what are farms for? Both questions require immediate and thoughtful answers from everyone who sees what is happening to land, water, food, animals, human beings, and culture.

My answers: Farms are our foundation for making our next evolutionary step. By restoring balance and making the land and waters vibrantly healthy, the Earth's sacred dimension is more clearly revealed and strengthened in support of all life. With that radiant foundation we human beings can more readily fulfill what I feel our lives are for in this era: continuing to evolve from *homo sapiens* to *homo spiritus*.

The term *homo spiritus* refers to what many writers have identified as our next and necessary evolutionary step: women and men who have awakened and who also grasp the fundamental fact of our connection with each other, the Earth, and all the forms of life upon the Earth. This is not an abstract or unattainably lofty goal of perfection but rather, as Dennis Klocek articulates in this chapter's epigram, a fundamental requirement for survival.

Many people and many groups are actively exploring the question of what farms are for, through a range of creative farm and food initiatives and networks, not just in North America but around the world. This chapter cites just a few of these initiatives by way of example, but an internet search will reveal a cornucopia of possibilities and models. More particularly, this chapter explores the rising agroecological vision—in the Americas and around the world—that deep agroecology aspires to help clarify and unify.

Basic Human Need—When she wrote *Key Concepts of Environmental Education* for the United Nations Environment Program, Donella Meadows (1941–2001) included a section titled "Sacredness." "Material needs are basic," she wrote. "Their absence threatens survival, and without survival no higher human goal can even be considered. But the moment that survival is assured, the next question becomes survival for what?"

Meadows, a founder of the Balaton Group and lead author of *The Limits to Growth* (1972), raised core questions about the quality of life and ultimate reasons for human existence. "A healthy, beautiful environment is not a luxury," Meadows stipulated, "it is a basic human need, both materially and non-materially." An insightful systems thinker and an early supporter of both organic growing systems and Community Supported Agriculture (CSA), Meadows' contributions continue to influence agroecology and deep agroecology.

A Living Organism—During a phone conversation in 2015, farmer John Peterson of Angelic Organics (Farmer John) told me, "A farm is not just an economic unit to produce food. It's also a living social, environmental, and educational organism. It cannot be thought of as just a unit of economic production. That just commodifies the farms and farmers, as food is commodified also."

Beauty and Joy—"If we do not permit the Earth to produce beauty and joy, it will in the end not produce food either," wrote Joseph Wood Krutch.

Leaving a Worthy Legacy—One thing farms are definitely for is for leaving a legacy of fundamental goodness and beauty for the next seven generations. That's a lofty goal, a laudable aspiration. We must hope that it is the kind of aspiration with the potential to give people a deep feeling of pride and well-earned honor for having taken part in reaching toward the goal, individually and collectively. That's establishing a worthy legacy. That kind of soul focus is a powerful inspiration for people to "walk in beauty, live in beauty," as our Navajo relatives remind us through their poetic prayers. It's also a judicious response to the question, *what are people for?*

Natural Beauty—The author of *Silent Spring,* Rachel Carson (1907–1964), wrote, "I believe natural beauty has a necessary place in the spiritual development of any individual or any society. I believe that whenever we substitute something man-made and artificial for a natural feature of the earth, we have retarded some part of man's spiritual growth."

A Sacrament—"To live, we must daily break the body and spill the blood of Creation. When we do this knowingly, lovingly, skillfully, reverently, it is a sacrament. When we do it ignorantly, greedily, clumsily, destructively, it is a desecration," agrarian elder Wendell Berry observed.

First Step—A first step in addressing the realm of nature is to deepen our understanding of the whole and the web of corresponding relationships that constitute the whole. We have much to gain from penetrating the mysteries via science and intuition and much to contribute in response. Dogma stands between us and our capacity to apprehend and comprehend what spirit is revealing in any instant of time. Time in nature, open to direct experience of it, enables us to cross the threshold.

Culture of Life—At the Mountain West Seed Summit in 2017 I heard Andrew Kimbrell speak. Director of the Center for Food Safety, he said, "We face the spiritual challenge of moving from a culture of death to a culture of life."

How to make that move? The native wisdom teachings of this land, as I understand them, counsel us on a fundamental level to spend time in nature. Look down at the earth. Look up at the sky. Feel what's going on. Allow yourself to be touched by what is alive and in relation. One might also actively consider, really, where your food comes from. Does our financial investment in food for ourselves and our household square up with our values and ethics? Not knowing—unconsciousness—is no excuse in a critical era. To not examine or consider is to make a choice.

Thanksgiving—Admiration of and appreciation for farms and farmers is important, not just in the sense of building morale but also in the sense of building a powerful, coherent field of energy within and around the farm and the community of human beings who make it happen.

Admiration is a feeling of respect and approval, sincere esteem that is conveyed energetically in giving thanks by the light of our thoughts and emotions. It's an authentic quality of energy transmitted by the stream of biophotons emitted from our thoughts and feelings.

In addition to the men and women who are our farmers, plants also sense admiration and benefit from it; that point was made decades ago by Peter Tompkins and Christopher Bird in *The Secret Life of Plants*. That book presented a wide array of scientific evidence showing the complex relationship between plants and human beings. Well received even by skeptics, the book offered many documented scientific insights into the nature of life itself and the multifaceted energetic interplay between people and plants. Plants like and benefit from our caring attention.

When a crowd cheers for the home team, an invisible wave of sound and emotional energy is transmitted to the players, who generally respond with greater energy and effort. Likewise, when an audience applauds, the invisible wave of appreciation and admiration warms and rewards the performer. The invisible can be felt. Animals feel appreciation and admiration, too. We all feel admiration when it is sincere, and of course sometimes when it's insincere. When the admiration is true, we are strengthened by it. In this manner, honest admiration is a worthwhile soul state to cultivate in relation to our attitudes and actions around farms, farmers, forests, and seas. They need our beneficent admiration and engagement.

Imagination—Mark Twain famously said, "You can't depend on your eyes when your imagination is out of focus." Yet imagination is often in the modern context regarded as fantasy or delusion, while the word has other specific meanings that are altogether purposeful. One of those meanings has to do with the capacity to hold an image in the mind and the cultivated ability to hold that image with discernment, clarity, and strength. In this manner it is easier to come into right relationship with the elemental forces at work in the fields, orchards, yards, all the natural world.

As with any human capacity, imagination can be developed with practice, to enable insightful perceptions concerning what needs to happen in regard to a parcel of land. When rightly engaged, human imagination has the capacity to participate cooperatively with the elemental forces in any particular place. Elemental forces can communicate with us, and we with them, through images, or pictures, that arise.

Much in the way a musician imagines a song or a symphony before realizing it or a painter imagines a painting before beginning brushwork, so farming and gardening are creative spiritual acts that proceed from imagination.

Our Covenant with the Seeds—At the 2017 Mountain West Seed Summit I met Clayton Brascoupe, a Mohawk/Anishnabeg farmer based at Tesuque Pueblo in northern New Mexico. He's founder of the Traditional Native America Farmers Association.

"What is a seed?" Brascoupe asked in his remarks. "Seed is life, mother, embryo, treasure, potential, possibility, relative, our child. All of those things. There is a fundamental, essential relationship that we have… We've been going along side by side with each other for thousands of years, and now we are in this present generation.

"We have a treaty, a covenant with the seeds," he said. "The seeds are a part of who we are. We have to take care of our relatives, the seeds, and they in turn will take care of us. Seeds are the first link in the food chain, and this link is now under threat. Our responsibility is to preserve them for forthcoming generations. Seeds are the foundation not just of our food system, but of civilization itself."

Wise Eating—Eating steady quantities of processed food not only renders people more susceptible to cancer, as long-term research shows, it also creates for many people a kind of mental fog, a dullness that they may come to think of as their natural state. To move from mental fog to clarity is, in our century, a spiritual act of survival. It's something everyone can do, but it requires will and discipline. As is often said, every dollar we spend on food—whether in the market or in a restaurant—is a vote we cast on the kind of food system we have, the kind of system we support financially. Good or bad, those systems provide the sustenance for our physical health and mental clarity, as well as the state of the environment. There's a direct connection among all.

In recognition of the role our food money plays, the Center for Good Food Purchasing in the US has begun programs in major cities using the power of procurement (purchasing) to create a transparent and equitable food system that prioritizes the health and well-being of people, animals, and the environment. Los Angeles, Chicago, and San Francisco have adopted the program, and it has the potential to expand significantly.

Touch the Earth—Coming into direct physical relationship with the earth is stabilizing. Whether that means occasionally walking upon the land with bare feet, or stretching out on your back or stomach on a lawn, or resting against a tree, all these ways and more are grounding. They stabilize human beings.

This teaching was first shared with me in the late 1980s by Grandmother Twylah Nitsch (1913–2007) at her home on the Cattaraugus Reservation in western New York State. She told me that whenever I was feeling greatly stressed, or was upset with sadness or rage or any other consuming emotion, to go and lie upon the land.

"Mother Earth never denies any of her children," Grandmother told me. "She comforts all. In a time of great or even chaotic change, when stress is high, the earth will hold us, stabilize us, and strengthen us if we will but reach out to her."

Genius Loci—This Latin phrase refers to the pervading atmosphere or character of a particular place. *Genius loci* is also a term for naming the overlighting or protecting spirit of a place. If one is respectfully in touch with that spirit, pathways of communication open up, not with words but with images or gusts, or in other nonlinear unfoldments. In this way it is possible to consult the *genius loci* of a particular place and to initiate right relationship.

Baleful Elements—Haudenausenee elder Doug George-Kanentiio (Mohawk) has commented publicly on the subject of baleful elements. In teaching partnership with his wife, Joanne Shenandoah, Doug has explained how his people recognize that all creatures, and also nonsentient objects, have a soul or life force. Traditionally they refer to this life force as *alunda*. All of the alundas of all of the beings and objects are part of a concert, a collective existence.

He tells of traditional teachings that warn there will come a time when humans become so disconnected from the alundas of the Earth they forsake the teachings of the Great Law of Peace, which teaches respect for the natural fact of our inseparable oneness with nature. At the time of this disconnection, he has explained, humankind's disrespect of the Earth will lead to pollution of both sky and stream, paving the way for the "dark dragons" to escape from their prisons below the surface of the Earth.

Kanentiio regards the image of dragons trapped below the Earth's crust as a metaphor for fossil fuels. A product of hundreds of thousands of years of subterranean compression, oil and other fossil fuels are derived from great dinosaurs and plants of the ancient past. To get at this decayed dragon stuff, hydraulic fracturing (fracking) injects massive quantities of high-pressure water and chemicals into underground shale deposits. This process fractures the land, thereby enabling the extraction of oil and gas.

Troubling earthquake swarms respond to the intrusion. Then also are baleful elements released. The systematic pouring of killing chemicals upon farm fields year after year has a similar baleful impact.

The emergence of baleful elementals from deep within the Earth is manifestly ungood. The consequences are destabilizing of the planet. "If you go into the earth and extract these beings," Kanentiio has warned, "it brings about consequences."

Interdependent—"All ethics so far evolved rest upon a single premise: that the individual is a member of a community of interdependent parts. The land ethic simply enlarges the boundaries of the community to include soils, waters, plants and animals, or collectively the land," observed Aldo Leopold in "The Land Ethic" from *A Sand County Almanac*.

In Concert with the Cosmos—Pat Frazier of Peace and Plenty Farm in Colorado drove down to speak with our New Mexico biodynamic farming and gardening group in early autumn 2016. She told our group that the basic idea of biodynamics is to farm in concert with the cosmos.

"Being informed about the cosmos," she said, "helps us to be in harmony with the cosmos. The substance of the earth is only one breath away from the spirit of the earth. In a sense, biodynamic preparations are saying to the

forces, the elementals: 'you are invited and will be protected. We will continue to nurture you.'" She said that use of
the biodynamic preparations can bring benefits, such as
helping to increase the amount of organic matter in the
soil, accentuating the water-holding capacity of the soil,
and increasing the healthy diversity of plants and insects.

In a later phone conversation for this book, Frazier,
who also serves as board chair for the Josephine Porter
Institute, suggested backing up conceptually. "In striving
to understand our rightful place on Earth," she said, "our
first introduction to that as human beings is the context
in which we live. Most humans frame their reference from
what they can see, touch, hear, smell, and feel on a daily
basis. Ecology represents something that is tangible. So
that's a starting place for human beings to interact with
the planet that they are living on. Give and take. When
people start to engage our planet in a way that allows the
planet to connect reciprocally through give and take, then
you are making the leap from ecology and agroecology to
deep agroecology."

"We are changing the ecology of the world in a way,"
she said. "It's an evolutionary step. It boils down to the
knowledge that the Earth is a spiritual being that is kin-
dred with us. Human stewardship of the Earth can maintain things for a time, but if we don't take our work on
the land and our farms out to a cosmic level, then we are

missing a crucial evolutionary step. It's a step that we are sorely lacking in already. We need to make that leap."

We Know Enough Already—If we are going to address the challenges of climate change, water shortages, general resource depletion, human health, and all the other things, then the current industrial model of agriculture and food systems requires transformation into the models presented in true agroecology. We already know enough to establish a clear direction of travel: A wholesale transition to diversified agroecological systems must become the guiding principle for food systems reform.

Farmers Cannot Do It Alone—If we want to transform the global industrial agribusiness models to models of agroecology and deep agroecology, we'll have to step forward to work for change in our own communities. It's too much to ask of farmers—around 1 percent of the population in the US at this point—to carry the full responsibility of touching the earth on behalf of everyone to bring forth our sustenance.

Many people and many communities are already stepping forward. Local citizens, for example, saying "no" to more factory farms. Local communities saying "no" to pesticides. Voters asking tough questions about food and agriculture when considering which candidates to support for local offices. We need a lot more of this in many more places. At the same time, we need local community initiatives to continue coming forward and networking.

Local food policy councils are playing a key role as development laboratories for agricultural and food projects in regions all over North America, and more widely in the world.

Power of Local Networks—If your mission is transformation of something—like, say, our food and farming system—then there are many lessons to be learned from perhaps the most powerful creature in nature, the ant.

Stanford University professor Deborah M. Gordon writes about the intricate behavior of ants and the power of local networks. Turns out that we human beings would do well to emulate the ways in which individual ants connect locally to build extensive colonies—advice that couldn't be more relevant in times when we face overwhelming challenges when it comes to influencing national food, farming, and climate policies.

In her article, "Local Links Run the World," she notes, "Networks in nature show how, for the networks that we engineer and those that tie us to each other, the pattern of links at the local scale sets the options for stability and transformation. Almost everything that happens in life is the result of a network. Making, or breaking, local links is the way to change."

Leadership—"Every movement for human freedom throughout history has needed people to lead, people who stand for love and for higher law. That's the challenge we face now. That is what we need," said Dr. Vandana Shiva during her talk in Kansas City, Missouri, in 2014.

Food Democracy—The Pesticide Action Network (PAN) North America has defined food democracy in these terms: "...food democracy emphasizes fulfillment of the human right to safe, nutritious food that has been justly produced. It means ordinary people getting together to establish rules that encourage safeguarding the soil, water, and wildlife on which we all depend. It is also pragmatic politics built around the difficult lesson that food is too important to leave to market forces—that we all have a right and responsibility to participate in decisions that determine our access to safe, nutritious food."

Alliances—The United States Food Sovereignty Alliance (USFSA) is a network of food-justice, faith-based, food-producer, labor, environmental, and community groups. They are allied to end poverty, to rebuild local food economies, to assert democratic control over the food system, and to work toward ending poverty and disrespect for the human beings who grow food for the nation and the world.

The alliance's member organizations include Farm Aid, Pesticide Action Network, Food First, Food Chain Workers Alliance, Friends of the Earth, the Presbyterian Hunger Program (PHP), the Indigenous Environmental Network, the National Family Farm Coalition, La Via Campesina, and many more.

USFSA asserts that all people have the right to healthy, culturally appropriate food, produced in an ecologically sound manner. They work to uphold the right to food as a basic human need, and they work to connect both local and national struggles to the broader international movement for food sovereignty. Canada, Mexico, and many other nations have parallel networks, accessible through internet searches.

Indigenous peoples formed the Native American Food Sovereignty Alliance in 2013. A network for collaboration, NAFSA is set up to become a sustainable and organized movement that is Native American driven and controlled, dedicated to addressing food security, hunger, and nutrition.

Something We Are Proud Of—The Union of Concerned Scientists has published online a 50-State Food System Scorecard. This is an innovative effort to establish a comprehensive set of indicators about each state's food system. The vision that led them to create the scorecard is itself an expression of the values that in general are motivating agroecological food systems work.

In the preamble to the scorecard, the scientists write: "From farm to fork, our food system should be something we are proud of—supporting farmers, workers, and local economies; ensuring that everyone has access to enough nutritious food to stay healthy; and protecting our soil and water for the future."

Consilience Enhances Resilience—Agroecology is a multidisciplinary field that includes economics and social science as well as traditional science. Harvard biologist E. O. Wilson refers to this kind of interconnectedness among disciplines as "consilience." The term agroecology itself, one could say, describes the consilience of agriculture, ecology, and several other disciplines.

While preparing a talk for the 2015 Midwest CSA farm conference, I inevitably encountered the word *resilience* and soon found myself musing about its possible relation to *consilience,* a word with a similar sound.

Resilience is about the strength and flexibility that allows people and systems to endure shocks or adversity—such as climate chaos—and yet still be able to reorganize to keep functioning. Consilience describes linking together principles from different disciplines, especially when forming a comprehensive theory or system. It's a convergence of independent insights and capacities.

In realms such as science, history, and computer networks, consilience has been appreciated for some time. But the concept is fitting as well for deep agroecology, the systems we use to bring forth our essential food, wood, and fiber from the land, and the need to enhance their resilience.

Adaptation for Global Stability—We're in a time when the idea expressed by that odd combination of words (consilience enhances resilience) is, in fact, essential. According to the US National Intelligence Council's 2012 project report *Global Trends 2030*, global stability will be threatened in the years immediately ahead of us by changing climate, volatile markets, and wars. Meanwhile, the USDA's landmark 2015 report *Climate Change, Global Food Security, and U.S. Food System* concludes that climate change is likely to affect global, regional, and local food security. It will drive an overall increase in food prices and disrupt food availability.

That's a grim outlook. But the USDA report also states that adaptation can make a positive difference. That's where households and communities of all sizes and constellations need to place their attention and their energy. We must respond to our circumstances or be overwhelmed. Locally and globally we absolutely require intelligent strategies to adapt, to reduce our vulnerability, to build resilience, to reckon with the increasing disruptions of climate change and geopolitics, and to evolve spiritually.

Community Supported Agriculture (CSA)—CSA farms are promising agroecological models, models with a track record of creative collaboration (consilience) to enhance resilience. CSA farms are local partnerships between farmers and the households of human beings in a formal supportive relationship with the farm. Through their very existence, CSA farms are responding to and exploring the question *what are farms for?* They may serve as a prototype for a new social contract between farmers and the people they feed.

Community farms now involve well over a million people in communities all around the globe, from the United States and Canada to Asia, Europe, Africa, and beyond. CSAs are anchored in neighborhood communities in cities, suburbs, and countryside, all constellated around local agroecological farms. Those farms are producing healthy, diversified, and high-quality nutritious food and regenerated soils. With many thousands of farms serving as models for addressing the current global food challenges, the CSA movement continues to develop.

Through global associations, such as URGENCI, the international network for community-supported agriculture, CSA provides a pathway for people to come together and to pool their intelligences, their energies, and their resources in a practical community venture that builds food security and resilience while helping to heal the land. CSA is a model adaptable to needs and resources of any given community, but generally adhering to some guiding principles: responsible care for soil, water, and seeds through agroecological principles; food as a common good rather than a commodity; human-scale producing rooted in local realities and knowledge; fair working conditions and income for all involved; respect for the environment; and humane animal welfare.

Precondition of Our Lives—In the early 1990s I had the opportunity to partner with Trauger Groh (1932–2016) in coauthoring the first book about CSA, *Farms of Tomorrow: Community Supported Farms, Farm Supported Communities*. One set of the ideas Trauger articulated in the book struck me as a key realization for deep agroecology: "Farming is not just a business like any other profit-making business, but a precondition of human life on earth. As such, farming is everyone's responsibility. Our intention is to share the experience of farming through CSA with everyone who understands that our relationship with nature and the ways we use the land will determine the future of the earth.

"Community supported agriculture is not just another new and clever approach to marketing.

Rather, CSA is about the necessary renewal of agriculture through its healthy linkage with the human community that depends on farming for survival. CSA is also about the necessary stewardship of soil, plants, and animals: the essential capital of human cultures... That farms flourish must be the concern of everyone, not just the individuals working as farmers."

Co-ops—Food co-ops are a major web of market nodes in the overall agroecological, good food movement. They are owned independently by the people who shop in them, local citizens in cities and towns across the nation who make a modest investment as shareholders and thereby become member-owners. For many decades, food co-ops have provided a principal connection between families who want clean, chemical-free food and the stalwart network of sustainable organic farmers who provide it. Although they face great challenges, co-ops are a leading edge for agroecology and deep agroecology.

Food Politics—As a five-year member of the board of directors for Open Harvest Coop Grocery in Lincoln, Nebraska, I had the opportunity to learn about co-op ideals and practices. Our co-op did business with well over a hundred local farms, directly helping them to stay on the land and in business.

In the summer of 2012 I traveled to Philadelphia for the 56th annual convention of the Consumer Cooperative Management Association (CCMA). They are the network hub for about 128 of America's food co-ops. Marion Nestle was a keynote speaker on the final day of the conference.

A long-time nutrition activist and author of several influential books, including *Food Politics*, Nestle began with a blunt statement: "There is a global food crisis right now, with one in seven people on the Earth already hungry." Nestle said that it looks as if the global food crisis will continue to intensify in the years immediately ahead. And she said that in the years ahead we would likely see the crisis play out not just with overseas famines but also domestically in the cost, volatility, and availability of food.

"Hunger and malnutrition are social problems," Nestle said, "and that is one of the reasons why food co-ops are so important. Co-ops are a viable alternative to Big Food. Because co-ops are both community based and value based, they make a point of selling clean, healthy, nutritious food."

Humane—Robert Karp, former director of Practical Farmers of Iowa and of the Biodynamic Association, offered some pertinent observations during a visit to Santa Fe in May 2018. He said industrial agriculture tends to treat soil and plants like mechanisms, with strict material formulas for manipulation and performance. Likewise, he said, industrial systems tend to treat animals like plants—confining them so that they, essentially, cannot move, and cannot express their fundamental animal nature. Thus, one way we can be better is by supporting the humane treatment of farmed animals, to ensure that they are allowed to express their inherent nature.

We See What Is Happening—At the 2017 Mountain West Seed Summit in Santa Fe, Beata Tsosie-Peña of Santa Clara Pueblo observed: "We cannot wait for science to validate the harm we know is happening... I urge you to listen deeply to the struggle and voices of global indigenous communities who are currently putting their lives on the line to protect what they hold sacred. Their defense of the sacred places is important for the well-being of the whole Earth."

Nodes in the Matrix—Certain places on Earth have long inspired and blessed people. In every generation, and from all the world's cultural and spiritual traditions, pilgrims have sought out these holy places: Santiago de Compostela in Spain, Varanasi in India, Stonehenge, Mecca, Notre Dame, Machu Picchu, and Jerusalem, for examples. These are but a few of the thousands of sites of unusual power and mystery. In a broader conception, they are energy nodes in a vast matrix of earth energies that pervade and encircle our planet. Farms are likewise part of that matrix, and they can help strengthen it.

Lakota Chief Arvol Looking Horse, Keeper of the White Buffalo Calf Woman Pipe, has eloquently encouraged people to respectfully visit sacred sites. He emphasizes that for the well-being of our Earth, this is important. I've crossed paths with Arvol a number of times over the years: First in Eugene, Oregon, then with a circle of elders at UN Headquarters on Manhattan, with Reuben Snake, Jr. on the Winnebago Reservation in Nebraska, and most memorably during ceremony in the hogan of Navajo Grandfather Martin Martinez (1910–2006) on his ranch in Haystack, New Mexico. The eagle staff ceremony progressed over four days. One afternoon as a pipe went around the circle, four horses cantered up to the door of the hogan to look in at Looking Horse, then dashed away. I saw and I knew (*Vidi et Scio*).

As a spokesperson for many native people, Looking Horse has designated June 21 of each year (summer solstice) as *World Peace and Prayer Day* to help people focus attention on making pilgrimage to special places. Tradition keepers say that no matter where you are upon the Earth, there is a sacred place within a day's journey. According to Looking Horse, visiting these nodes—the sacred sites—intelligently and respectfully can help restore overall planetary balance. That overall balance is essential for our climate, our farms, our food, and our health.

Chief Looking Horse has reached out inclusively: "Our vision is for the peoples of all continents, regardless of their beliefs in the Creator, to come together as one at their Sacred Sites to pray and meditate and commune with one another, thus promoting an energy shift to heal our Mother Earth and achieve a universal consciousness toward attaining peace."

Main Chance—The phrase *main chance* generally refers to the most advantageous prospect available, the opportunity for the greatest gain. William Shakespeare employed the phrase memorably in a speech by the Earl of Warwick in *Henry VI, Part 2*:

> "*There is a history in all men's lives,*
> *figuring the nature of the times deceased,*
> *the which observed,*
> *a man may prophesy, with a near aim,*
> *of the **main chance** of things as yet not come to life...*"

With my nearest aim, I now prophesy for the future that our *main chance* would be wisely grasped in reference to collective ambitions that we must of necessity awaken in ourselves: ambitions for survival, for health, for well-being, for a clean Earth, for respect, for purpose, for the next seven generations, for beauty, for spiritual maturity. All of this is what farms are for. They are the key to our physical, moral, and spiritual survival and evolution. Our main chance to realize all of this lies in the realms of agroecology and deep agroecology.

Acknowledgments

Arne Naess (1912–2009) was a treasured Norwegian philosopher who took the basic idea of ecology to another level by conceiving of deep ecology. His work is of ongoing value and an inspiration for deep agroecology. Chuck Francis is the person who first spoke the words "deep agroecology" to me. Those two words set me on a quest to draw together the ancient and emerging threads I have followed in my writing career: native knowings and agrarian wisdom ways. Thank you, Professor Francis, for setting me on a path of learning. Any observations in this book that critique people or institutions are mine alone.

Brazilian scholars Maria Izabel Vieira Botelho, Irene Maria Cardoso, and Kei Otsuki authored the first published mention of the term deep agroecology. Their paper, "'I Made a Pact with God, with Nature, and with Myself'": Exploring Deep Agroecology," was published in November 2015 in the journal *Agroecology and Sustainable Food Systems*.

I thank my wife, Elizabeth Wolf, for uncountable deeds of inspiration and support. This book is dedicated to her. Our homes have been in Nebraska and New Mexico; thus, readers will find various location shifts as they make their way through the book.

For attention to detail, accuracy, and artistry, I thank cover designer Angela Werneke of River Light Media in Santa Fe and layout wizards Cris Trautner and Aaron Vacin of Infusionmedia in Lincoln.

I offer my heartfelt thanks to the many farmers and earth patriots of the world—the wide-ranging communities of human beings who tend the earth with love and wisdom. Their plentiful insights are woven into this book. They are worthy of honor. I extend my respect, appreciation, and gratitude to a wide circle of friends, acquaintances, and fellow agrarians for their influence, for their insights, and for their support.

Everyone named in *Deep Agroecology* has made an important contribution, for which I am grateful. Many dozens of others have also contributed to my understanding via books, articles, talks, debates, and friendships: Trauger and Alice Bennet Groh, Lincoln Gieger, Anthony Graham, John S. Mercer, Carolyn Clay Mercer-McFadden, Cynthia Walker, Leon Secatero, Shawn Secatero, Vangee Nez, Emigdio Ballon, Luisa Elena Kolker, Wes Jackson, Joel Salatin of Polyface Farm, Stephen Clarke and Juli Ferrara, Chris Peters, Reuben Snake, Jr., Bill Watkinson, Wounded Bear, Dennis Meadows and Suzanne Mac-Donald, Debbie Stroh, Bill Pfeiffer, Andrew Rothovius,

Woody Wodraska and Barbara Victoria Scott, Gail Larsen, Ellen Kleiner, Elizabeth Henderson, Judith Hitchman, Dee and Sammie Justesen, Michael Pollan, Laura Lengnick, Jim Pathfinder Ewing, Belle Starr, Bill McDorman, LeeAnn Hill, Tom Philpott, Mark Bittman, Allan Balliett at Fresh & Local CSA, Doug Dittman at Branched Oak Farm, Evrett Lunquist and Ruth Chantry at Common Good Farm, Alex McKiernan and Chloe Diegel at Robinette Farm, JD Tarwater, Charla Hermann, the Balaton Group, The Cornucopia Institute, Food First, Beneficial Farms CSA in Santa Fe, Open Harvest Coop Grocery in Lincoln, the Nebraska Sustainable Agriculture Association, Buy Fresh Buy Local Nebraska, La Montanita Coop, the Biodynamic Association, Rebecca Briggs, Sarah Weber, Robert Karp, Thea Maria Carlson, the New Mexico Biodynamic Group, the Santa Fe Farmers Market Institute, the Food & Environment Reporting Network (FERN), contributors to the COMfood email list, and more.

The many voices raised in this book arise from citation or conversation. In approximate order of appearance in the text: the Haudenausenee authors of *Basic Call to Consciousness*, Miguel Altieri, Wendell Berry, Leon Shenandoah, Eric Holt-Giménez, Andrew Kimbrell, John Ikerd, La Via Campesina, Blain Snipstal, James Hansen, Olivier De Schutter, Paolo Manzelli, C. G. Jung, Albert Einstein, Fritz-Albert Popp, Richard Ford, Brant Secunda and

Los Huicholes, Charles L. Sanders, Paul D. MacLean, Tom Robbins, Carlos Barrios, Don Alejandro Cirilo Perez, Alan Oken, Arthur Ashkin, Sir James Jeans, Bruce Lipton, Iona Miller, Lynn McTaggart, Gary Schwartz, Hugh Lovel and Shabari Bird, David Spangler, Aristotle, Theophrastus, George Sessions, Dolores LaChapelle, The Land Institute, Thomas Spaulding, Farmer John Peterson, Angelic Organics, Vandana Shiva, FAO, Rudolf Steiner, FERN (Food and Environment Reporting Network), Wolf Song, Wayne Pacelle, Brooke Medicine Eagle, Tanah Whitemore, Severine T. Fleming, AmyLee, Matias Baker, Larry Little Bird, Winona LaDuke, Sun Bear, Eunice Baumann-Nelson, Lynn Ghel, Beata Tsosie-Peña, Emigdio Ballon, Joanne Shenandoah and Doug George-Kanentiio, Barbara Alice Mann, Manitonquat (Medicine Story), Robin Wall Kimmerer, William Commanda, James Lovelock, Lynn Margulis, Joseluis Ortiz, Matias Baker, Bruno Follador, Eduardo Rincon, Hunbatz Men, Alberto Taxo, Dennis Klocek, Patricia Anne Davis, Donella Meadows, Debbie Stroh, Joseph Wood Krutch, Slow Turtle (John Peters), Rachel Carson, Christopher Bird, Peter Tompkins, Clayton Brascoupe, Yehwenode (Twylah Nitsch), Ross Jennings, Aldo Leopold, Pat Frazier, Deborah M. Gordon, Elizabeth Henderson, Marion Nestle, Enso Nastati, and Arvol Looking Horse. Thank you, one and all.

Sources

Introduction

Abbott, Chuck. "Midwest Farmers Uproot FDR's 'Great Wall of Trees.'" Food and Environmental Reporting Network (FERN), thefern.org. November 1, 2017.

Bailey, Liberty Hyde. *The Holy Earth: The Birth of a New Land Ethic.* Dover Publications. 2009.

Case, Anne and Sir Angus Deaton. "Mortality and Morbidity in the 21st Century." *Brookings Papers on Economic Activity.* Washington, DC: Brookings Institution Press. March 23, 2017.

Haudenosaunee (Iroquois) elders. *Basic Call to Consciousness: The Haudenosaunee Address to the Western World. Akwesasne Notes*, ed. First published in 1978. Summertown, TN: Native Voices Books, 2005.

Itzkan, Seth, Karl Thidemann, and Bill McKibben. "Using Soil to Fight Climate Change." *Rutland Herald* (Rutland, VT). March 25, 2017.

Jung, C. G. *The Earth Has a Soul: The Nature Writings of C. G. Jung.* Sabini, Meredith, ed. Berkeley: North Atlantic Books, 2002.

Kauffman, Jonathan. "Growing Concern: Organic Farms Need a New Generation to Keep Them Alive." *San Francisco Chronicle*, sfchronicle.com. August 21, 2017.

McFadden, Steven. "Historic Pivot Point for Food Democracy." Deep Agroecology blog. April 24, 2014. https://deepagroecology.org/2014/04/

Ohliger, Erica and Nelson Caraballo. "Remembering Our Sacred Place in Nature: The Mother Earth Restoration Trust." *Green Fire Times* (Santa Fe, NM). August 2017. https://greenfiretimes.com/2017/08/remembering-our-sacred-place-in-nature-the-mother-earth-restoration-trust/

Tsosie-Peña, Beata. "A Tewa Woman's Reflection on Urgency." Tewa Women United website. November 2017. http://tewawomenunited.org/a-tewa-womens-reflection-on-urgency/

Washington Post Editorial Board. "Americans are Dying 'Deaths of Despair.' Will Trump Help?" The Post's View. *The Washington Post*. March 25, 2017.

Chapter 1: Right Names

Common Dreams. "Pope Francis Joins Battle Against Transgenic Crops." August 2015. http://www.commondreams.org/news/2015/08/12/pope-francis-joins-battle-against-transgenic-crops

Davenport, Coral. "Major Climate Report Describes a Strong Risk of Crisis as Early at 2040." *The New York Times*. October 7, 2018.

FAO, IFAD, UNICEF, WFP and WHO. *The State of Food Security and Nutrition in the World 2018: Building Climate Resilience for Food Security and Nutrition.* Rome: FAO. 2018. https://www.who.int/nutrition/publications/foodsecurity/state-food-security-nutrition-2018/en/

The Free Dictionary/Legal Dictionary. "Greed" definition. Retrieved March 20, 2019. https://legal-dictionary.thefreedictionary.com/greed

Gandhi, Mahatma. *The Collected Works of Mahatma Gandhi*. New Delhi: Publications Division, Ministry of Information and Broadcasting, Government of India, 2001.

Gore, Al. *An Inconvenient Sequel: Truth to Power*. Emmaus, PA: Rodale Books, 2017.

Holt-Giménez, Eric. "Overcoming the Barrier of Racism in Our Capitalist Food System." *Food First Backgrounder* 24, no. 1 Spring 2018. Oakland, CA: Food First/Institute for Food and Development Policy.

Intergovernmental Science-Policy Platform on Biodiversity and Ecosystem Services (IPBES), "Global Assessment of Biodiversity and Ecosystem Services." May 2019. https://www.ipbes.net

Kolbert, Elizabeth. *The Sixth Extinction: An Unnatural History*. New York: Henry Holt & Co., 2014.

Larkin, Molly. "What is the Seventh Generation Principle and Why Do You Need to Know About It?" Molly Larkin blog. http://www.mollylarkin.com/what-is-the-7th-generation-principle-and-why-do-you-need-to-know-about-it-3/

Pope Francis. Encyclical "Laudato Si." May 24, 2015. http://www.nytimes.com/interactive/2015/06/18/world/europe/encyclical-laudato-si.html?_r=0

Ripple, William J., and 15,364 scientist signatories from 184 countries. "World Scientists' Warning to Humanity: A Second Notice." *BioScience*. November 13, 2017. https://academic.oup.com/bioscience/article/67/12/1026/4605229

Willet, Walter, M.D., et al. "Food in the Anthropocene: The EAT-Lancet Commission on Healthy Diets from Sustainable Food Systems." January 2019. https://www.thelancet.com/commissions/EAT

Chapter 2: Industrial Farms and Food

Abarca-Gómez, Leandra, et al. "Worldwide Trends in Body-mass Index, Underweight, Overweight, and Obesity from 1975 to 2016: A Pooled Analysis of 2,416 Population-based Measurement Studies in 128.9 Million Children, Adolescents, and Adults." *The Lancet* 390, no. 10113, 2627–42, October 10, 2017.

Arsenault, Chris. "Only 60 Years of Farming Left If Soil Degradation Continues." Rome: Thompson Reuters Foundation. December 5, 2014. https://www.scientificamerican.com/article/only-60-years-of-farming-left-if-soil-degradation-continues/

Bar-On, Yinon M., Rob Phillips, and Ron Milo. "The Biomass Distribution on Earth." *Proceedings of the National Academy of Sciences of the United States of America* 115, no. 25, 6506–11, May 21, 2018. DOI: 10.1073/pnas.1711842115

Bercik, P., E. F. Verdu, and S. M. Collins. "Is Irritable Bowel Syndrome a Low-grade Inflammatory Bowel Disease?" *Gastroenterology Clinics* 34, issue 2, 235–45. June 2005. https://www.ncbi.nlm.nih.gov/pubmed/15862932

Bottemiller Evich, Helena. "The Great Nutrient Collapse: The Atmosphere Is Literally Changing the Food We Eat, for the Worse. And Almost Nobody is Paying Attention." *Politico.* September 13, 2017. https://www.politico.com/agenda/story/2017/09/13/food-nutrients-carbon-dioxide-000511

Breitburg, Denise, et al. "Declining Oxygen in the Global Ocean and Coastal Waters." *Science* 359, issue 6371. January 5, 2018. https://science.sciencemag.org/content/359/6371/eaam7240.full

Commission on Genetic Resources for Food and Agriculture. *The State of the World's Biodiversity for Food and Agriculture, Assessments.* Food and Agriculture Organization of the United Nations (FAO). 2019. http://www.fao.org/cgrfa/topics/biodiversity/sowbfa/en

Consumer Reports. "Special Report: Eat the Peach, Not the Pesticide." March 19, 2015. http://www.consumerreports.org/cro/health/natural-health/pesticides/index.htm

Fiolet, Thibault, et al. "Consumption of Ultra-processed Foods and Cancer Risk: Results from NutriNet-Santé Prospective Cohort." *British Medical Journal* 360. February 14, 2018. DOI: 10.1136/bmj.k322

Food and Agriculture Organization of the United Nations (FAO) website. "Livestock and the Environment." Accessed May 12, 2018. http://www.fao.org/livestock-environment/en/

Gallagher, James. "Ultra-processed Foods 'Linked to Cancer'." *BBC News: Health.* February 15, 2018. http://www.bbc.com/news/health-43064290

Ghabbour, Elham A., et al. "National Comparison of the Total and Sequestered Organic Matter Contents of Conventional and Organic Farm Soils." *Advances in Agronomy* 146, 1–35. 2017. https://www.sciencedirect.com/bookseries/advances-in-agronomy/vol/146/suppl/C

Gilbert, Natasha. "One-third of our Greenhouse Gas Emissions Come from Agriculture." *Nature: International Weekly Journal of Science.* October 31, 2012. http://www.nature.com/news/one-third-of-our-greenhouse-gas-emissions-come-from-agriculture-1.11708

GMWatch. "Scientists Warn of Toxic Chemical Cocktail Sprayed on Food." November 22, 2017. https://www.gmwatch.org/en/news/latest-news/17988

Hagai, Levine, et al. "Temporal Trends in Sperm Count: A Systematic Review and Meta-regression Analysis." *Human Reproduction Update* 23, issue 6, 1–14. July 25, 2017. DOI:10.1093/humupd/dmx022

Hakim, Danny. "Doubts About the Promised Bounty of Genetically Modified Crops." *The New York Times.* October 29, 2016.

Hallmann, Caspar, et al. "More than 75 Percent Decline over 27 Years in Total Flying Insect Biomass in Protected Areas." *PLoS ONE* 12, no. 10. October 2017. DOI: 10.1371/journal.pone.0185809

Harvey, Chelsea. "This Tiny Moth is Stirring up the GMO Debate in New York." *The Washington Post.* November 20, 2015. https://www.washingtonpost.com/news/energy-environment/wp/2015/11/20/this-tiny-moth-is-stirring-up-the-gmo-debate-in-new-york/?utm_term=.92657b6ab688

Hebrew University of Jerusalem, The. "Significant Ongoing Decline in Sperm Counts of Western Men." *Human Reproduction Update.* July 26, 2017. Accessed at www.sciencedaily.com/releases/2017/07/170726110954.htm

Helbring, Dirk, et al. "Will Democracy Survive Big Data and Artificial Intelligence?" *Scientific American.* February 25, 2017. https://www.scientificamerican.com/article/will-democracy-survive-big-data-and-artificial-intelligence/?wt.mc=SA_Twitter-Share

Hilbeck, Angelika, et al. "No Scientific Consensus on
    GMO Safety." *Environmental Sciences Europe* 27, no.
    4. January 24, 2015. DOI: 10.1186/s12302-014-
    0034-1

Ikerd, John. JohnIkerd.com. "The Economic Coloniza-
    tion of Rural America: Increasing Vulnerability in a
    Volatile World." August 2017. http://johnikerd.com/
    the-economic-colonization-of-rural-america-increas-
    ing-vulnerability-in-a-volatile-world/

InterAcademy Partnership. *Opportunities for Future Re-
    search and Innovation on Food and Nutrition Security
    and Agriculture: The InterAcademy Partnership's Global
    Perspective.* Trieste, Italy. November 2018.

International Panel of Experts on Sustainable Food
    Systems (IPES-Food). *Unravelling the Food-Health
    Nexus: Addressing Practices, Political Economy, and
    Power Relations to Build Healthier Food Systems.* Com-
    missioned by the Global Alliance for the Future of
    Food. September 2017. http://www.ipes-food.org/
    reports/

—. *Too Big to Feed: Exploring the Impacts of Mega-merg-
    ers, Consolidation and Concentration of Power in*

the Agri-food Sector. October 2017. http://www. ipes-food.org/reports/

—. *From Uniformity To Diversity. A Paradigm Shift from Industrial Agriculture to Diversified Agroecological Systems.* June 2016. http://www.ipes-food.org/reports/

James, Ian, and Steve Reilly. "Pumped Beyond Limits, Many U.S. Aquifers in Decline." Four-part series for *USA Today* and *The Desert Sun.* December 2015. https://www.desertsun.com/story/news/environ-ment/2015/12/10/pumped-beyond-limits-many-us-aquifers-decline/76570380/

Johnson, Kristina. "Pesticides and Plastics to Blame in Plummeting Sperm Counts." *FERN's Ag Insider.* August 2017. https://thefern.org/ag_insider/

Lancet, The. *The Global Syndemic of Obesity, Undernu-trition and Climate Change: The Lancet Commission Report.* January 27, 2019. DOI: 10.1016/S0140-6736(18)32822-8

Larsen, Ashley E., et al. "Agricultural Pesticide Use and Adverse Birth Outcomes in the San Joaquin Valley of California." *Nature Communications* 8,

article number: 302. August 29, 2017. DOI:
10.1038%2Fs41467-017-00349-2.ris

Lassale, Camille, et al. "Healthy Dietary Indices and Risk
of Depressive Outcomes: A Systematic Review and
Meta-analysis of Observational Studies." *Molecular
Psychiatry*. September 2018. DOI: 10.1038/s41380-
018-0237-8

Latham, Jonathan. "Unsafe at any Dose? Diagnosing
Chemical Safety Failures, from DDT to BPA." *Independent Science News*. May 16, 2016. https://www.
independentsciencenews.org/health/unsafe-at-any-
dose-diagnosing-chemical-safety-failures-from-ddt-
to-bpa/

—. "There's Nothing Parochial about the Issue of GMO
Food Labeling." *Independent Science News*. January
24, 2017. https://www.independentsciencenews.org/
health/theres-nothing-parochial-about-the-issue-of-
gmo-food-labeling/

—. "Gene Drives: A Scientific Case for a Complete and
Perpetual Ban." *Independent Science News*. February
13, 2017. https://www.independentsciencenews.
org/environment/gene-drives-a-scientific-case-for-a-
complete-and-perpetual-ban/

Liang, Xin-Zhong, et al. "Determining Climate Effects on US Total Agricultural Productivity." *Proceedings of the National Academy of Sciences of the United States of America* 114, no. 12, E2285–92. March 21, 2017. DOI: 10.1073/pnas.1615922114

MacDonald, Fiona. "Hidden 'Dead Zones' in the Ocean Have Quadrupled Since the '50s, and That's Really Bad." *Science Alert.* January 5, 2018. https://www.sciencealert.com/dead-zones-in-ocean-quadrupled-since-1950s-killing-marine-life

MacDonald, James M., Robert Hoppe, and Doris Newton. "Three Decades of Consolidation in U.S. Agriculture." *Economic Information Bulletin* 189, USDA. March 2018. https://www.ers.usda.gov/publications/pub-details/?pubid=88056

MacIssac, Tara. "A Diet High in Pesticides May Be Poisoning America. Safety Limits for Food Don't Account for How Pesticides Mix Together and Accumulate in the Body." *The Epoch Times.* October 26, 2017. https://www.theepochtimes.com/a-diet-high-in-pesticides-may-be-poisoning-america-2_2339671.html

McFadden, Steven. "Rivulets of Revelation Flow from Tales of Two Farm & Food Conferences." Deep Agroecology blog. May 17, 2011. https://deepagroecology.org/2011/05/17/rivulets-of-revelation-flow-from-tales-of-two-conferences/

—. "No No Nano: Macro-objections to Micro-machinations of Industrial Processed Food." Deep Agroecology blog. October 2, 2014. https://deepagroecology.org/2014/10/02/no-no-nano-macro-objections-to-micro-machinations-of-industrial-processed-food/

McIntosh, W. L., et al. "Suicide Rates by Occupational Group—17 States, 2012." *Morbidity and Mortality Weekly Report* 65, 641–45, 2016. DOI: 10.15585/mmwr.mm6525a1

Milner, Alice M. and Ian L. Boyd. "Toward Pesticidovigilance." *Science*. 1232–34. September 22, 2017. DOI: 10.1126/science.aan2683

New York Times Editorial Board, The. "Insect Armageddon." *The New York Times*. Oct. 29, 2017.

Rabin, Roni Caryn. "Cancer Group Calls for Colorectal Cancer Screening Starting at Age 45." *The New York Times.* May 30, 2015.

—. "More Young People are Dying of Colon Cancer." *The New York Times.* August 22, 2017.

Richtel, Matt, and Andrew Jacobs. "How Big Business Got Brazil Hooked on Junk Food." *The New York Times.* September 16, 2017.

Ridlington, Elizabeth, Elizabeth Berg, Matt Wellington, and Kara Cook-Schultz. *Reaping What We Sow: How the Practices of Industrial Agriculture Put Our Health and Environment at Risk.* U.S. PIRG Education Fund and Frontier Group. February 7, 2018. https://uspirgedfund.org/reports/usp/reaping-what-we-sow

Rohling, Eelco, and Joseph Ortiz. "We're Killing Our Lakes and Oceans. The Consequences Are Real." *Undark Magazine.* February 6, 2018. https://undark.org/article/dead-zones-oceans-lakes-coastal-seas/

Sánchez-Bayo, Francisco, and Kris A. G. Wyckhuys. "Worldwide Decline of the Entomofauna: A Review of its Drivers." *Biological Conservation* 232, 8–27, April 2019. DOI: 10.1016/j.biocon.2019.01.020

Sanderman, Jonathan, Tomislav Hengl, and Gregory J. Fiske. "Soil Carbon Debt of 12,000 Years of Human Land Use." *Proceedings of the National Academy of Sciences of the United States of America* 114, no. 36, 9575–80, August 21, 2017. DOI: 10.1073/pnas.1706103114

Shetterly, Caitlin. *Modified: GMOs and the Threat to Our Food, Our Land, Our Future.* New York: G. P. Putnam's Sons, 2016.

Siegel, Rebecca L., Kimberly D. Miller, and Ahmedin Jemal. "Colorectal Cancer Mortality Rates in Adults Aged 20 to 54 Years in the United States, 1970-2014." Research Letter. *Journal of the American Medical Association.* August 8, 2017. http://jamanetwork.com/journals/jama/article-abstract/2647859?result-Click=1

Subcommittee on Ecological Systems, Committee on Environment, Natural Resources, and Sustainability of the National Science and Technology Council. *The State and Future of U.S. Soils: Framework for a Federal Strategic Plan for Soil Science.* December 2016. https://obamawhitehouse.archives.gov/sites/default/files/microsites/ostp/ssiwg_framework_december_2016.pdf

United States Environmental Protection Agency website. "Sources of Greenhouse Gas Emissions: Agricultural Sector Emissions." Accessed October 15, 2018. https://www.epa.gov/ghgemissions/sources-green-house-gas-emissions#agriculture

University of Nebraska–Lincoln. "Two Major U.S. Aquifers Contaminated by Natural Uranium: Naturally Occurring Uranium is Being Mobilized by Farm-related Pollution." Accessed April 4, 2019. *Science Daily.* www.sciencedaily.com/releases/2015/08/150817132508.htm

Weingarten, Debbie. "Why are America's Farmers Killing Themselves in Record Numbers?" *The Guardian.* December 6, 2017. https://www.theguardian.com/us-news/2017/dec/06/why-are-americas-farmers-killing-themselves-in-record-numbers

Chapter 3: Elements of Agroecology

Alliance for Food Sovereignty in Africa and Tanzania Organic Agriculture Movement. *Agroecology: The Bold Future of Farming in Africa.* Dar es Salaam, Tanzania, 2016. http://afsafrica.org/wp-content/uploads/2017/02/

Agroecology-the-bold-future-of-farming-in-Africa-ebook1.pdf

Alteri, Miguel A. *Agroecology: The Science of Sustainable Agriculture*, 2nd edition. Boulder, CO: Westview Press, 1995.

— and Clara I. Nicholls. "Agroecology: A Brief Account of Its Origins and Currents of Thought in Latin America." *Agroecology and Sustainable Food Systems* 41, no. 3-4, 231–37, 2017. DOI: 10.1080/21683565.2017.1287147

Baudry J., K. E. Assmann, M. Touvier, et al. "Association of Frequency of Organic Food Consumption with Cancer Risk Findings from the NutriNet-Santé Prospective Cohort Study." *JAMA Internal Medicine* 178, no. 12. October 2018. DOI: 10.1001/jamainternmed.2018.4357

Bekoff, Mark. *The Emotional Lives of Animals: A Leading Scientist Explores Animal Joy, Sorrow, and Empathy— and Why They Matter*. Novato, CA: New World Library, 2007.

Binder, Karen. "Agroecology more than a Farming System." A report on a talk by John Ikerd at the Organic

Grain Growers Conference. *AgriNews Publications*. February 8, 2018. http://www.agrinews-pubs.com/news/agroecology-more-than-a-farming-system/article_0531f779-77b5-52d4-9994-89c381a470ff.html

Brown, Corie. "Rural Kansas is Dying: I Drove 1,800 Miles to Find Out Why." *The New Food Economy*. April 26, 2018. https://newfoodeconomy.org/rural-kansas-depopulation-commodity-agriculture/

Caporali, Fabio. "Agroecology as a Transdisciplinary Science for a Sustainable Agriculture." Chapter in *Biodiversity, Biofuels, Agroforestry and Conservation Agriculture*. Ed. Eric Lichtfouse. Sustainable Agriculture Reviews book series (SARV, volume 5). 2010. DOI: 10.1007/978-90-481-9513-8_1

Coté, Charlotte. "'Indigenizing' Food Sovereignty: Revitalizing Indigenous Food Practices and Ecological Knowledges in Canada and the United States." *Humanities* 5, no. 57. Basel, Switzerland. July 15, 2016. DOI: 10.3390/h5030057

De Schutter, Olivier. "Report of the Special Rapporteur on the Right to Food—Final Report: The Transformative Potential of the Right to Food." *UN General*

Assembly, Human Rights Council. January 24, 2014.
http://www.srfood.org/en/documents

Cultivate! Book reviews of *Food Sovereignty, Agroecology, and Biocultural Diversity: Constructing and Contesting Knowledge.* Ed. Michel P. Pimbert. Routledge, 2018.
http://www.cultivatecollective.org/in-perspective/
new-book-on-biocultural-diversity-and-knowl-
edge-democracy/

Food and Agriculture Organization of the United Nations (FAO) website. "Agroecology Knowledge Hub."
http://www.fao.org/agroecology/en/

Forum for Food Sovereignty. "Declaration of Nyéléni."
February 27, 2007. https://nyeleni.org/IMG/pdf/
DeclNyeleni-en.pdf

Francis, Charles, et al. "Agroecology: The Ecology of
Food Systems." *Journal of Sustainable Agriculture* 22,
no. 3, 99–118, 2003. DOI: 10.1300/J064v22n03_10

Gliessman, Steve. "A Brief History of Agroecology in
Spain and Latin America." *Agroecology and Sustainable Food Systems* 41, no. 3-4, 229–30, 2017. DOI: 10
.1080/21683565.2017.1292390

Global Justice Now website. "Six Pillars of Food Sovereignty." Developed at the international forum held in Nyéléni, Mali, Africa, on February 27, 2007. Accessed May 13, 2019. https://www.globaljustice.org.uk/six-pillars-food-sovereignty

Hansen, James, et al. "Young People's Burden: Requirement of Negative CO_2 Emissions." *Earth System Dynamics* 8, 577–616, 2017. DOI: 10.5194/esd-8-577-2017

Henderson, Elizabeth. "Principles of Organic Agriculture and of Organic 3.0 in the US and Canada." *ThePryingMantis.com.* 2018.

—. *Building Organic Bridges: Report from the IFOAM Organic World Congress 2014.* Published on the website of the National Organic Coalition. Nov. 6, 2014.

Ikerd, John. "Agroecology: Science, Social Movement, or Farm Management?" Keynote address at the Organic Grain Conference hosted by The Land Connection. Champaign, Illinois. February 1, 2018.

Khadse, Ashlesha. *Women, Agroecology & Gender Equality.* New Dehli: Focus India Publications. July 2017. Accessed at https://red-liess.org/wp-content/

uploads/2017/10/women_agroecology_gender_
equality.pdf

Latham, Jonathan. "Why the Food Movement is Un-
stoppable." *Independent Science News*. September 20,
2016. https://www.independentsciencenews.org/
health/why-the-food-movement-is-unstoppable/

La Via Campesina. *Peasant Agroecology for Food Sovereignty and Mother Earth*. La Via Campesina Study
Booklet, No. 7. November 2015. https://viacampesi-
na.org/en/peasant-agroecology-for-food-sovereign-
ty-and-mother-earth-experiences-of-la-via-campesi-
na-now-available/

Lengnick, Laura. *Resilient Agriculture: Cultivating Food
Systems for a Changing Climate*. Gabriola Island, British Columbia: New Society Publishers, 2015.

Moss, Daniel, and Mark Bittman. "Bringing Farming
Back to Nature." *The New York Times*. June 26, 2018.

Pimbert, Michael P., ed. *Food Sovereignty, Agroecology,
and Biocultural Diversity: Constructing and Contesting Knowledge*. Centre for Agroecology, Water and
Resilience (CAWR), Coventry University, United
Kingdom. November 2017.

Rosset, Peter M., and Miguel A. Altieri. *Agroecology: Science and Politics.* Agrarian Change and Peasant Studies Book 7. Nova Scotia, Canada: Fernwood Books Ltd., 2017.

Snipstal, Blain. "Toward a 'People's' Agroecology." March 29, 2016. https://whyhunger.org/category/blog/towards-a-peoples-agroecology/

Third World Network and Sociedad Cientifica Latino-americana de Agroecologica (SOCLA). *Agroecology: Key Concepts, Principles and Practices: Main Learning Points from Training Courses on Agroecology held in Solo, Indonesia (5-9 June 2013) and Lusaka, Zambia (20-24 April 2015).* Accessed May 13, 2019 at http://twn.my/title2/books/Agroecology.htm

Wezell, A., et al. "Agroecology as a Science, a Movement and a Practice. A Review." *Agronomy for Sustainable Development* 29, no. 4, 503–15, October 2009. DOI: 10.1051/agro/2009004.

Wikipedia. "Precautionary principle" entry. Accessed May 13, 2019. https://en.wikipedia.org/wiki/Precautionary_principle

World Bank. *International Assessment of Agricultural Knowledge, Science and Technology for Development (English). Global Program Review* 4, no. 2. Washington, D.C.: World Bank, 2010. http://documents. worldbank.org/curated/en/636821468316165959/ International-assessment-of-agricultural-knowledge-science-and-technology-for-development

Chapter 4: Webs of Light and Life

Afshordi, Niayesh, et al. "From Planck Data to Planck Era: Observational Tests of Holographic Cosmology." *Physical Review Letters* 118, no. 4, July 2016. DOI: 10.1103/PhysRevLett.118.041301

Becker, Adam. *What is Real? The Unfinished Quest for the Meaning of Quantum Physics.* New York: Basic Books, 2018.

Best, Shivali. "Scientists Have Stored Light as Sound for the First Time in a Breakthrough that Could Lead to Super-fast Computers." *The Daily Mail.* September 19, 2017. https://www.dailymail.co.uk/sciencetech/ article-4898576/Scientists-transfer-light-sound-waves-world-first.html

Crowther, Thomas W., et al. "Biotic Interactions
    Mediate Soil Microbial Feedbacks to Climate
    Change." *Proceedings of the National Academy of
    Sciences of the United States of America*, May 18, 2015.
    DOI: 10.1073/pnas.1502956112

Castells, Manuel. "Informationalism, Networks, and
    The Network Society: A Theoretical Blueprint."
    Published in *The Network Society: A Cross-Cultural
    Perspective*. Ed. Manuel Castells. Northampton, MA:
    Edward Elgar, 2004.

Emerging Technology from the arXiv. "Biophoton
    Communication: Can Cells Talk Using Light?" *MIT
    Technology Review*. May 22, 2012. https://www.tech-
    nologyreview.com/s/427982/biophoton-communi-
    cation-can-cells-talk-using-light/

George-Kanentiio, Doug. Facebook posting. March 18,
    2019. Used with permission.

Goff, Philip, William Seager, and Sean Allen-Herman-
    son. "Panpsychism." *The Stanford Encyclopedia of Phi-
    losophy*, Winter 2017. Ed. Edward N. Zalta. https://
    plato.stanford.edu/archives/win2017/entries/pan-
    psychism/

Ho, Mae-Wan. "Iluminating Water and Life: Emilio Del Giudice." *Electromagnetic Biology and Medicine.* 34, no. 2, 113–122. June 22, 2015. DOI: 10.3109/15368378.2015.1036079

Jung, C. G. *Man and His Symbols.* New York: Dell Publishing, 1968.

Lipton, Bruce. "An Introduction to Spontaneous Evolution." Recorded by Hay House at the "I Can Do It!" Conference, 2010. www.brucelipton.com.

MacLean, Paul D. *The Triune Brain in Evolution: Role in Paleocerebral Functions.* New York: Plenum Press, 1990.

McElhinney, M. W. and W. E. Senanayake. "Paleomagnetic Evidence for the Existence of the Geomagnetic Field 3.5 Ga Ago." *Journal of Geophysical Research*, 85, July 10, 1980. DOI: 10.1029/JB085iB07p03523

McFadden, Steven. "Steep Uphill Climb: Messages from the Mayan Milieu." Chiron Communications blog, 2002. https://chiron-communications.com/chirons-cave/passages-essays-reports-and-profiles-by-steven-mcfadden/steep-uphill-climb-messages-from-the-mayan-milieu/

McTaggart, Lynne. *The Intention Experiment: Using Your Thoughts to Change Your Life and the World.* New York: Atria Books. 2008.

Miller, Iona. "Photonic Human: My Zero Point." Photonic Human website. Accessed May 15, 2019. https://photonichuman.weebly.com/

Mullaney, James. *Celebrating the Universe: The Spirituality & Science of Stargazing.* New York: Hay House, 2013.

Overbye, Dennis. "Nobel Prize in Physics Awarded to Scientists Who Put Light to Work." *The New York Times.* October 2, 2018. https://www.nytimes.com/2018/10/02/science/physics-nobel-prize.html?emc=edit_na_20181002&nl=breaking-news&nlid=47943027ing-news&ref=cta

Popp F. A., et al. "Biophoton Emission: New Evidence for Coherence and DNA as a Source." *Cell Biophysics* 6, issue 1, 33–52, March 1984. DOI: 10.1007/BF02788579

— et al. "Physical Aspects of Biophotons." *Experientia* 44, no. 7, 576–85. July 15, 1988. https://www.ncbi.nlm.nih.gov/pubmed/3294033

Robbins, Tom. *Jitterbug Perfume*. New York: Bantam Books. 1984.

Steiner-Adair, Catherine, and Teresa H. Barker. *The Big Disconnect: Protecting Childhood and Family Relationships in the Digital Age*. New York: Harper Collins, 2013.

Sanders, Charles L. "Speculations about Bystander and Biophotons." Letter. *Dose-Response*, 12, issue 4, 515–17. May 19, 2014. DOI: 10.2203/dose-response.14-002.Sanders

Zarkeshian, Parisa, et al. "Are There Optical Communication Channels in Our Brains?" *MIT Technology Review*. September 6, 2017. https://www.technologyreview.com/s/608797/are-there-optical-communication-channels-in-our-brains/

Chapter 5: Elements of Deep Agroecology

Austin, Mary Hunter. *Earth Horizon: An Autobiography*. Literary Guild, 1932.

Botelho, Maria Izabel Veira, et al. "'I made a pact with God, with Nature, and with Myself': Exploring

Deep Agroecology." *Agroecology and Sustainable Food Systems* 40, issue 2, 116–131, November 2015. DOI: 10.1080/21683565.2015.1115798

Connolly, Christopher N. "Nerve Agents in Honey." *Science* 358, issue 6359, 38–9. October 6, 2017. DOI: 10.1126/science.aao6000

Drengson, Alan, and Yuichi Inoue. *The Deep Ecology Movement: An Introductory Anthology*. Berkeley, CA: North Atlantic Books, 1995.

Drengson, Alan, and Bill DeVall, eds., *The Ecology of Wisdom: Writings by Arne Naess*. Counterpoint Press, 2010.

Ewing, Jim Pathfinder. *Conscious Food: Sustainable Growing, Spiritual Eating*. Scotland: Findhorn Press, 2012.

Farrelly, Michael G., Clare Westwood (Third World Network), and Stephen Boustred (TOAM), eds. *Agroecology: The Bold Future of Farming in Africa*. AFSA Agroecology Working Group and Tanzania Organic Agriculture Movement, 2016. https://afsafrica.org/agroecology-the-bold-future-of-farming-in-africa/

Food and Agriculture Organization of the United Nations (FAO). *The State of Food and Agriculture: Women in Agriculture, Closing the Gender Gap for Development.* 2011. http://www.fao.org/publications/sofa/2010-11/en/

Fromartz, Sam. "Iconic Northwest Organic Produce Company Sold, Without Selling Out." *FERN's Ag Insider.* July 5, 2018. https://thefern.org/ag_insider/iconic-northwest-organic-produce-company-sold-without-selling-out/

Harwatt, Helen. "Including Animal to Plant Protein Shifts in Climate Change Mitigation Policy: A Proposed Three-step Strategy." *Climate Policy* 19, no. 5, 533–41. November 26, 2018. DOI: 10.1080/14693062.2018.1528965

InterAcademy Partnership. *Opportunities for Future Research and Innovation on Food and Nutrition Security and Agriculture: The InterAcademy Partnership's Global Perspective.* InterAcademy Partnership. Trieste, Italy. November 2018. https://www.interacademies.org/48898/Opportunities-for-future-research-and-innovation-on-food-and-nutrition-security-and-agriculture-The-InterAcademy-Partnerships-global-perspective

Jeans, Sir James. *The Mysterious Universe*. Cambridge, England: Cambridge University Press, 1931.

LaChapelle, Dolores. *Sacred Land, Sacred Sex, Rapture of the Deep: Concerning Deep Ecology and Celebrating Life*. Kivaki Press, 1988.

Land Institute, The. "A 50-Year Farm Bill." Proposed by The Land Institute, Salina, KS. June 2009. https://landinstitute.org/wp-content/uploads/2016/09/FB-edited-7-6-10.pdf

McFadden, Steven. "Rivulets of Revelation Flow from Tales of Two Farm & Food Conferences." Deep Agroecology blog. May 17, 2011. https://deepagroecology.org/2011/05/17/rivulets-of-revelation-flow-from-tales-of-two-conferences/

—. "Sacred Tobacco Teachings Illuminate Bee Colony Collapse Catastrophe." Deep Agroecology blog. April 23, 2011. https://deepagroecology.org/2011/04/23/sacred-tobacco-teachings-illuminate-bee-colony-collapse-catastrophe/

—. "Humane Husbandry: Nebraska Tries to Blaze a Trail." Deep Agroecology blog. July 25, 2013. https://deepagroecology.org/2013/07/

—. "Consilience Enhances Resilience: A Key Element of CSA Farms." Deep Agroecology blog. December 14, 2015. https://deepagroecology.org/2015/12/

—. "Prepping for Resilient Community: Wherever Two of More are Gathered." *Applied Biodynamics*, journal of the Josephine Porter Institute, issue 90, Fall/Winter 2016. Accessed at https://chiron-communications.com/prepping-for-resilient-community/

—. "Grafting the Food System to America's Rootstock." Chiron Communications blog. August 3, 2016. https://chiron-communications.com/grafting-the-food-system-to-americas-rootstock/

—. "Notes on the Mountain West Seed Summit." Blog essay for Chiron-Communications.com. March 5, 2017. https://chiron-communications.com/notes-mountain-west-seed-summit/

Pfeiffer, Bill. *Wild Earth, Wild Soul: A Manual for an Ecstatic Culture*. Moon Books, 2013.

Schieber, Hamutal. "2019 Food and Beverage Diet Trends: Protein, Vegan, Gut Health, Intermittent Fasting, Keto, CBD." *Schieber Research*. December 25,

2018. https://researchci.com/health-wellness-diet-trends-for-2019-protein-vegan-gut-health-intermittent-fasting-keto/

Sessions, George, ed. *Deep Ecology for the 21st Century: Readings on the Philosophy and Practice of the New Environmentalism*. Boston: Shambhala Publications, 1995.

Steiner, Rudolf. *Agriculture: Spiritual Foundations for the Renewal of Agriculture*. Biodynamic Farming & Gardening Association, 1993.

—. *Nature's Open Secret: Introductions to Goethe's Scientific Writings*. Classics in Anthroposophy series. Rudolf Steiner Press, 2010.

Shiva, Vandana. *Monocultures of the Mind: Perspectives on Biodiversity and Biotechnology*. Zed Books, 1993.

—. *Making Peace with the Earth*. Pluto Press, 2013.

Smith, Robert Leo, and Stuart L. Pimm. "Ecology" entry. *Encylopaedia Britannica*. Accessed January 18, 2018. https://www.britannica.com/science/ecology

Wodraska, Woody. *Deep Gardening: Soul Lessons from 17 Gardens, Biodynamic Memories.* Aurora Farm Publishing. 2010.

Zegler, Jenny, ed. "Global Food and Drink Trends 2019." Mintel Group, Ltd, 2018. https://www.mintel.com/global-food-and-drink-trends/

Chapter 6: This Is the Holy Land

Candelario, Elizabeth. "Dr. Mercola Interviews [Director of Demeter USA] on Biodynamics." YouTube video interview. October 9, 2017. https://youtu.be/vaf-1Ntd-XvI

Coté, Charlotte. "'Indigenizing' Food Sovereignty: Revitalizing Indigenous Food Practices and Ecological Knowledges in Canada and the United States." *Humanities* 5, no. 57. Basel, Switzerland. July 15, 2016. DOI: 10.3390/h5030057

Dominus, Susan. "When the Revolution Came for Amy Cuddy." *The New York Times.* October 22, 2017.

Brewer, John. "Oneida Library Hosts Program on Iroquois Myths, Legends and Prophecy." Report on talk by Doug George-Kanentiio. *Oneida Daily Dispatch*, January 14, 2017. https://www.oneidadispatch.com/news/oneida-library-hosts-program-on-iroquois-myths-legends-and-prophecy/article_98fefc35-2b47-59d7-a55c-566c33929287.html

Ghel, Lynn, *Claiming Anishinaabe: Decolonizing the Human Spirit*. Treaty 4 Territory, Saskatchewan, Canada: University of Regina Press, 2017.

Herman, William H., and Paul Zimmet. "Type 2 Diabetes: An Epidemic Requiring Global Attention and Urgent Action." *Diabetes Care* 35, no. 5, 943–44, May 2012. DOI: 10.2337/dc12-0298.

Intergovernmental Science-Policy Platform on Biodiversity and Ecosystem Services (IPBES). *Summary for Policymakers of the Global Assessment Report: Key Messages and Policy Options, as Approved by the IPBES Plenary*. May 4, 2019. bit.ly/IPBESReport

Kimmerer, Robin Wall. *Braiding Sweetgrass: Indigenous Wisdom, Scientific Knowledge, and the Teachings of Plants*. Minneapolis: Milkweed Editions, 2013.

Leopold, Aldo. *A Sand County Almanac*. Oxford, England: Oxford University Press, 1949.

Mann, Barbara Alice. *Iroquoian Women: The Gantowisas.* American Indian Studies Series Book 4. New York: Peter Lang Inc., International Academic Publishers, 2006.

McFadden, Steven. "This is the Holy Land." Deep Agroecology blog. May 22, 2010. https://deepagroecology.org/2010/05/

Robbins, Jim. "Native Knowledge: What Ecologists are Learning from Indigenous People." *Yale360 Environment.* April 26, 2018. https://e360.yale.edu/features/native-knowledge-what-ecologists-are-learning-from-indigenous-people

Chapter 7: Tierra Viva

Kimmerer, Robin Wall. *Braiding Sweetgrass: Indigenous Wisdom, Scientific Knowledge, and the Teachings of Plants.* Minneapolis: Milkweed Editions, 2013.

Klocek, Dennis. *Sacred Agriculture: The Alchemy of Biodynamics.* Great Barrington, MA: Lindisfarne Books, 2013.

Steiner, Rudolf. *The Human Heart*. Mercury Press, re-
    print edition. 1985.

Chapter 8: What Are Farms For?

Berry, Wendell. *What Are People For?* Berkeley: Counter-
    point Press, 2010.

Costa, Temra. *Farmer Jane: Women Changing the Way
    We Eat*. Layton, Utah: Gibbs Smith, 2010.

Groh, Trauger, and Steven McFadden. *Farms of Tomor-
    row Revisited: Community Supported Farms, Farm
    Supported Communities*. The Biodynamic Farming
    and Gardening Association, Inc., 1998.

Klocek, Dennis. *Climate: Soul of the Earth*. Great Bar-
    rington, MA: Lindisfarne Books, 2011.

Kurzweil, Ray. *The Age of Spiritual Machines: When
    Computers Exceed Human Intelligence*. New York:
    Penguin Books, 2000.

Lamb, Gary. "Community Supported Agriculture: Can
    it Become the Basis of a New Associative Economy?"
    Threefold Review 11, 39–44, 1994.

—. "The Fundamental Social Law: Theory and Practice." *Biodynamics*, Spring 2008.

—. *Associative Economics: Spiritual Activity for the Common Good*. Ghent, NY: The Association of Waldorf Schools of North America, 2010.

Leslie, Issac Sohn, and Monica M. White. "Race and Food: Agricultural Resistance in U.S. History." Chapter in *Handbook of the Sociology of Racial and Ethnic Relations*, eds. Pinar Batur and Joe R. Feagin. 347–64. June 2018. https://link.springer.com/chapter/10.1007/978-3-319-76757-4_19

Meadows, Donella H. *Harvesting One Hundredfold: Key Concepts and Case Studies in Environmental Education*. United Nations Environment Program (UNESCO-UNEP International Environmental Education Series), 1989. http://www.donellameadows.org/wp-content/userfiles/Harvesting-one-hundredfold.pdf

Organic Consumers Association. "Like an Ant." Blog post on Stanford University biology professor Deborah M. Gordon's article "Local Links Run the World." February 1, 2018. https://www.organicconsumers.org/newsletter/organic-bytes-577-just-dawn/ant

Pesticide Action Network North America (PAN)
    website. "Food Democracy." Accessed May 16, 2019.
    http://www.panna.org/key-issues/food-democracy

Poppen, Jeff. "Community Supported Agriculture and
    Associative Economics." *Biodynamics*, Spring 2008.

Schneider, Steffen, and Rachel Schneider. "Uncovering a
    New Narrative for Agriculture: Wendell Berry and
    Rudolf Steiner." Institute for Mindful Agriculture
    website. March 24, 2016. https://www.institutefor-
    mindfulagriculture.org/uncovering-a-new-narrative

Shannon, Kerry L., et al. "Food System Policy,
    Public Health and Human Rights in the United
    States." *Annual Review of Public Health* 36, 151–73,
    March 2015. DOI: 10.1146/annurev-publhealth-
    031914-122621

Steiner, Rudolf. *Towards Social Renewal: Rethinking the
    Basis of Society*. 4th revised ed. Originally published
    in German in 1923. London: Rudolf Steiner Press,
    1977.

Tompkins, Peter, and Christopher Bird. *The Secret
    Life of Plants: A Fascinating Account of the Physical,*

Emotional and Spiritual Relations Between Plants and Man. Harper & Row, 1973.

US Department of Agriculture. *Climate Change, Global Food Security, and U.S. Food System.* 2015. https://www.usda.gov/oce/climate_change/FoodSecurity.htm

US National Intelligence Council. *Global Trends 2030: Alternative Worlds.* December 2012. https://publicintelligence.net/global-trends-2030/

Index

About the Author

Independent journalist Steven McFadden has been writing about the Earth, farms, and food for decades. With Trauger Groh, he is coauthor of the first two books on Community Supported Agriculture (CSA): *Farms of Tomorrow: Community Supported Farms, Farm Supported Communities* (1990) and *Farms of Tomorrow Revisited* (1998). He's also the author of *The Call of the Land: An Agrarian Primer for the 21st Century* and *Awakening Community Intelligence: CSA Farms as 21st Century Cornerstones*.

He is the author of a contemporary epic, nonfiction saga of North America that is freely available online: *Odyssey of the 8th Fire* (www.8thfire.net). It tells a true story arising from the deepest roots of our land but taking place in the present and the future. In it, circles upon circles, elders of the Americas make a generous giveaway of the teachings they carry.

In the early 1990s, Steven served as director of The Wisdom Conservancy at Merriam Hill Education Center in Greenville, New Hampshire, and as the national coordinator for the annual 1993 Earth Day Celebration. In partnership with the Seventh Generation Fund, Steven helped develop the curriculum and launch the nationwide Council Circles program for community gatherings.

Steven's nonfiction books also include

Profiles in Wisdom
Teach Us to Number Our Days
Legend of the Rainbow Warriors
A Primer for Pilgrims
Native Knowings
Tales of the Whirling Rainbow
Classical Considerations

The author's websites:

DeepAgroecology.net
Chiron-Communications.com
8thFire.net

Selected Reviews of the Author's Books

About *The Call of the Land*
Independent Publisher: "The ecology of our planet and the health of its inhabitants is in peril, because we've lost our connection to the land. This book describes how we can rally to save the quality of our air, water and soil through a new agrarian revolution—starting at the local level to regain control of our food supply—and bring back a sane, intelligent, and holistic approach to the way we live on the land. Steven McFadden describes with eloquence and detail how it's already underway across the continent, and his book is a cornucopia of resources and ideas."

Journal of Agriculture, Food Systems, and Community Development: "Readers new to this movement sometimes struggle to identify a primer that is accessible and grounded in real-world examples. *The Call of the Land* lends itself as a tool for such readers, as it not only illustrates a foundational agrarian ethos historically argued by Wendell Berry and Wes Jackson, but it also outlines a variety of practical models and approaches to inform the practice of local food system development."

Courtney White, Quivira Coalition, New Mexico: *"The Call of the Land* is an important and timely primer on a resurgent agrarianism taking place around the nation. As the challenges of the 21st Century begin to bear down, we can take solace, and find pragmatic solutions, in the back-to-the-land work of progressive farmers, ranchers, conservationists, and many others. Hope dwells in the grassroots. This book is a great guide on where to look."

Farmer John Peterson, Angelic Organics: "In the face of widespread turmoil and resignation, *The Call of the Land* shows us that our hands, minds, and hearts, when used as one, are already healing ourselves and the planet earth. Steven McFadden reminds us that the seeds to a new future are being planted right now, that farms are Meccas of cultural and ecological renewal."

Ingrid Kirst, Community CROPS, Lincoln, Nebraska: *"The Call of the Land* will inspire you with page after page of innovative projects across the country that are having a positive impact on how we eat. Explore this comprehensive list of positive ideas and then implement them in your own community."

Teresa Opheim, Practical Farmers of Iowa: "It's inspiring to read about all of the wonderful efforts Steven McFadden details."

Charles Francis, UNL Center for Sustainable Agricultural Systems: "McFadden's call to action is clearly written and well referenced with a robust list of current websites and a bibliography for general reading on positive methods for resolving our food security challenge. Anyone interested in a good contemporary overview of challenges and solutions will find the book valuable."

Michael Faber, Monadnock Food Co-op, Keene, New Hampshire: "*The Call of the Land* workshop at Stonewall Farm was a great opportunity to forward our goals of producing a local, sustainable food system in our region."

About *Farms of Tomorrow*

Resurgence Magazine: "It is rare to come across any practical farming guide that sets out, from its inception, a set of principles that embrace social, spiritual and economic concerns on completely equal terms... The wisdom and clarity of philosophy are striking throughout."

Whole Earth Review: "This is the best book to access the Community Supported Agriculture (CSA) movement, including philosophical, spiritual, practical essays and how-to (including financial discussions). This is the source for tools, organizations, farms, and networks concerning the renewal of agriculture."

About *Profiles in Wisdom*
New York Times Book Review: "*Profiles in Wisdom* does a fine job not only of presenting the dignity, complexity, and wit of important Indian philosophers and religious leaders, but also of issuing cautions against easy uplift and wisdom injections. There are some stirring and unexpected powers unleashed in this book."

Library Journal: "This wise and provocative collection is highly recommended."

The Washington Times: "Our leaders should sit and listen to the counsel Steven McFadden has gathered in this book."

About *Legend of the Rainbow Warriors*
Odyssey Magazine: "I urge everyone on the spiritual path to read this small yet exceptionally powerful book."

Headline Muse: "In the wake of the September 11 tragedies, *The Legend of the Rainbow Warriors* is of added import. Clearly, human existence is experiencing profound shifts of consciousness... As one struggles to make sense of these recent events McFadden offers substantive insight and hope. Further, he speaks to the power of individuals to address the overwhelming and complex problems facing us today—locally as well as globally."

Critique Magazine: "To the uninitiated, reading *Legend of the Rainbow Warriors* is a bit like hearing one's native language spoken with an entirely new accent. The words are familiar, and the ideas and events of which he writes are certainly not news. But the light Mr. McFadden uses to illuminate his subject is alien. Self-sacrifice and stewardship of the land do not mix well with the American traditions of further, faster, and damn the consequences. Indeed, the juxtaposition of American-style progress and Native American sensibilities is one of history's oddest coincidences..."

About *Tales of the Whirling Rainbow*
Midwest Book Review, Editor's Choice: "Absorbing, engaging, thoughtful, thought-provoking, exceptionally well written, and thoroughly 'reader friendly' in organization and presentation, *Tales of the Whirling Rainbow* is unreservedly recommended for personal reading lists, as well as community and academic library collections."

Made in the USA
Middletown, DE
21 September 2021

48033757R00166